FINDERS KEEPERS LOSERS WINNERS

TRUE STORIES OF CHANGED LIVES

Kay Gray

Exulon Elite

Copyright © 2016 by Kay Gray

Finders Keepers Losers Winners
True Stories Of Changed Lives
by Kay Gray

Printed in the United States of America.

Edited by Xulon Press

ISBN 9781498471572

All rights reserved solely by the author. The author guarantees all contents are original and do not infringe upon the legal rights of any other person or work. No part of this book may be reproduced in any form without the permission of the author. The views expressed in this book are not necessarily those of the publisher.

Scripture quotations taken from the New International Version (NIV). Copyright © 1973, 1978, 1984, 2011 by Biblica, Inc.™. Used by permission. All rights reserved.

www.xulonpress.com

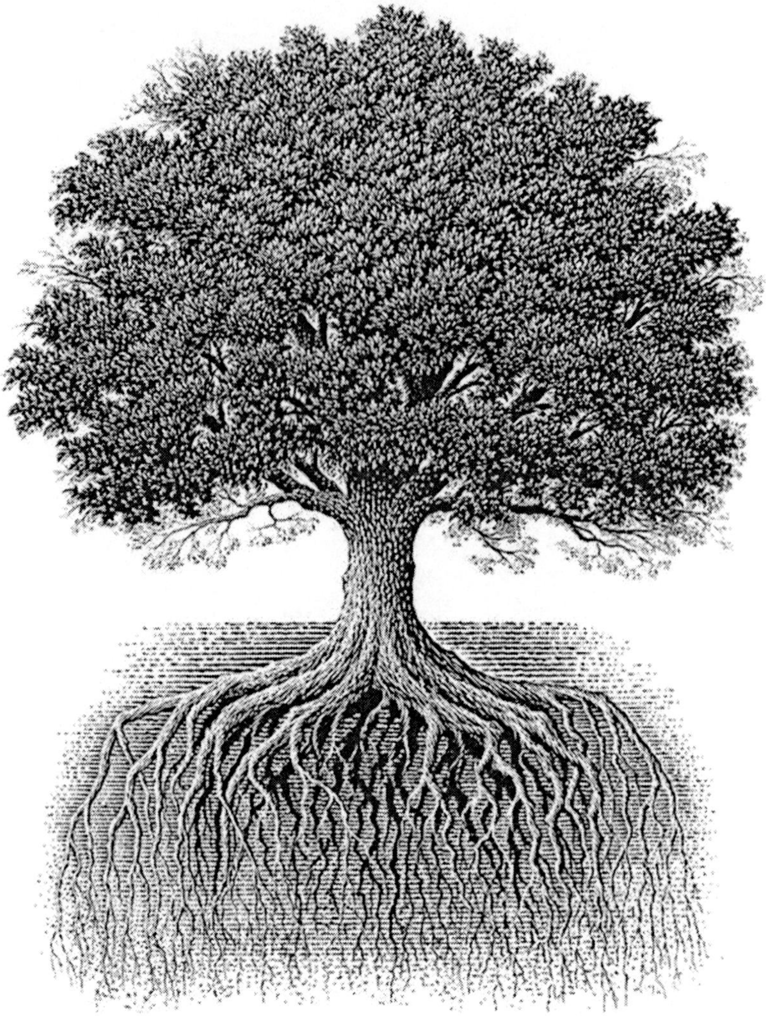

Psalm 1

Blessed is the man
Who does not walk in the counsel of the wicked
Or stand in the way of sinners
Or sit in the seat of mockers.
But his delight is in the law of the Lord,
And on his law he meditates day and night.
He is like a tree planted by streams of water
Which yields its fruit in season
And whose leaf does not wither.
Whatever he does prospers.
Not so the wicked!
They are like chaff
That the wind blows away.
Therefore the wicked will not stand in the judgment,
Nor sinners in the assembly of the righteous.
For the Lord watches over the way of the righteous,
But the way of the wicked will perish.

TABLE OF CONTENTS

1. DASH TO THE HOUSE........................9
2. NEVER CEASE TO BE AMAZED...........17
3. REWIND TO CRESTVIEW...................26
4. FRETTING FOR NAUGHT...................33
5. DAY IN THE LIFE................................41
6. ALL WORK AND NO PLAY?................48
7. SEASON OF HOPE.............................53
8. THE SURPRISE LISTENER..................58
9. FAMILY OF GOD................................65
10. JOSHUA..74
11. MEET YOU AT THE MORTUARY............82
12. NOT MY WAY, BUT HIS......................87
13. SLOW BUT STEADY WINS..................93
14. SIDE TRIP..104
15. HEART FOR MISSIONS....................113
16. WHERE HE CALLS, THEY GO...........121
17. VISITOR FROM THE PAST................126
18. LET'S HAVE A BURGER...................130

19.	A WIFE'S HEART	137
20.	MINISTRY TO WOMEN	143
21.	DESIRE TO MARRY	149
22.	THE OLD MAN SPEAKS WISDOM	155
23.	A CALL ON HIS LIFE	160
24.	WILD RIDE	171
25.	TRIO OF TROUBLE	176
26.	SMALL WORLD	181
27.	THE SEARCH FOR SELF	187
28.	THE SPRITE	192
29.	TRANSITION HOUSE STORY	200
30.	NEVER OUR OF SATAN'S REACH	205
31.	GOD DIRECTS OUR PATHS	214
32.	GOD ANSWERS PRAYER	219
	GREAT IS THY FAITHFULNESS	223
	FINAL THOUGHTS FROM THE AUTHOR	225
	ACKNOWLEDGEMENTS	227
	RESOURCES	231

DASH TO THE HOUSE

"Wait a minute!" I said as I turned to dash back into the house. How many times has God asked that very thing of me, even to the point of conveying to me, *"Be still, and know that I am God,"* (Ps. 46:10). You see, God has been a directing force in my life ever since I can remember. You might say that He has been my loving Father from the beginning, but that's another story. How little did I realize, at that very moment as I rushed back into the living room to get my Bible, that God, my Father, was beginning another adventure in my life following His plan.

There by my recliner was the Bible in the black leather satchel. I loved reading it more than my other Bibles because the size of the print made it so reader friendly on these not-so-young eyes. It had become my companion at Bible studies since it mysteriously found its way to my office a few years before. Tonight it was to accompany me on the beginning of a new path at my Father's prodding.

"Got it," I said to my new neighbor and friend, Paul, who waited patiently at the door during my impulsive dash back inside. "I wanted to take my Bible to church with us tonight. Just makes it easier to follow that good teaching," I smiled. Then, I noticed Paul had his Kindle Fire tucked under his arm, and I almost reneged on taking my Bible since I had a Kindle too. A quiet little feeling came over me that this Bible was supposed to go with us to church that Sunday evening, and so it did.

It was only my second visit to this Baptist church on Sunday evening. Ordinarily, Lutherans like me are content with Sunday morning services; however, the subject came up as Paul and I chatted in the front yard after walking our dogs a week before. Their church sign had indicated gospel singing at the church that Sunday. That sounded like fun to me, and I didn't hesitate when Paul asked me to accompany him. His famous last words were something like, "I'm not sure about the gospel music program, but if not you'll be in for some good Bible teaching by our youth minister."

Every word he uttered was true! We did miss the gospel music presentation, but I was invigorated by the direct and spirit-led teaching of the young minister, so much so that I was anxious to return the next week.

I recognized on the first visit how friendly and welcoming the parishioners were, so I was glad to meet and greet Paul's friends that I'd met the week previous. As we stood together chatting before the service, more friends of Paul's arrived. Diane and Ernie drew our attention to a group of at least twelve men that had entered the sanctuary and taken seats toward the front at the opposite side of the chapel. Diane was so full of joy in telling her story. It seemed the men were "disciples" at Oak Ridge Disciple House, a recovery program for addicts and alcoholics. Later I would come to know it as a Christian character building program. It was located about twenty miles from our town. Hearts and lives were turned over to Jesus at this residential center, and lives were being forever changed. My ears perked up when she said "Oak Ridge Disciple House" and I began to listen with greater interest. A mystery several years previous had been at the core of a futile search for this "Oak Ridge Disciple House."

Diane and Ernie had become involved with this ministry only recently but couldn't say enough about how God works in the lives of these men. Their son-in-law had recently completed the Oak Ridge program and was a truly changed man. Their joy and thankfulness was quite apparent in sharing the story.

"Was there a Mr. Harris, Joshua Harris, involved in that Oak Ridge House?" I interjected.

"Oh, yes!" Diane replied. "He was one of the founding forces in Oak Ridge and he has a truly amazing testimony of his own."

"But he passed away, didn't he?" I asked.

"Why no!" Diane exclaimed, "He's right there in the lavender shirt. He's sitting right behind the disciples." My eyes darted forward to rest on the man in the lavender shirt and I gazed at a young man about the age of my son.

"Oh my goodness," I said. My knees felt weak as I turned and sat down in the pew. "You're not going to believe this," I told them as I caught glimpses of confusion in the eyes of Paul and his friends. My hand reached quickly for my Bible. Hastily unzipping the cover and loosening the precious book from its confines, I held it up for the group to see. I didn't know what to say at first so I just held it up. There, on the cover of the Bible, was a name embossed in gold that had been a mystery to me for several years. The name was Joshua Harris!

As I faced my new friends, shivers ran through me and a quick realization that God was in charge of this new adventure. The looks on their faces were full of questions and I had a few answers to share but God would have to fill in the rest of the story. I spoke knowing time was short before the service began. "I used to own a boutique in Williamsburg Village. One day an employee came to my office requesting my presence at the dumpster out the back door. She said I wouldn't believe what she'd found when she took the trash out. We both peered into the dumpster and there among the rubble of daily discards were Bibles, devotional books, and flyers for Oak Ridge and cassettes along with some other personal belongings from some unknown soul. The precious Bible I carry tonight was among the findings we retrieved. Sybille and I both felt compelled to discover the story but couldn't understand why the word of God was in the trash. Upon going through the items further we found a letter written by some soul who was seemingly dying, relating his devastating addictions to drugs and alcohol. We arrived at the conclusion that someone has passed out of life and these were part of his belongings. Perhaps these were the belongings of Joshua Harris, the name on the Bible we found with the other Oak Ridge information. We were located down the way from Goodwill and it wasn't unusual to find items in our dumpster not accepted by Goodwill. But it was a mystery that haunted us and we just couldn't leave that beautiful Bible or those things in the dumpster."

"The disciples at Oak Ridge each write letters and die to their old selves as they find new life in Jesus," offered Diane. "They each place a cross in a burial area of the retreat when they do this." I thought, "Perhaps the letter I found was that of Joshua Harris." But I could tell that there was more to the story and more questions to be answered. And now even more believers were joining this journey with questions and awe. Our God is just an awesome God.

The service began and I whispered to Paul, "I must meet Joshua." He acknowledged my statement and agreed. My mind focused on the Scripture message as I followed along in Joshua's Bible. I smiled knowing that the man now worshipping across the way was the one responsible for all the notes and underlining in this text.

The service came to a close with a prayer and a hymn. My eyes followed Joshua as he accompanied the minister to an individual who had responded to an altar call. Then he strode back to his group. "Oh, Lord, I have to meet this man," I prayed.

As others gathered their belongings and began to leave the sanctuary, I sat and whispered a quick prayer. "Father, I don't know what is going on here and where you are leading, but I acknowledge your direction and willingly follow. Please reveal to me your will and let me do that which is good and right in your sight. And, oh God, bless the words of my mouth as I approach this stranger with what must be his Bible. Bless his heart to receive my story. And, I know this Bible is his and I must return it, but I've really become attached to it as my favorite study Bible. Bless me that I may do what is right and honorable in your sight. Amen."

"I've got to catch him," I said to Paul explaining my rush to the opposite side of the church. "I'm with you. I wouldn't miss this," replied Paul. Quickly we made our way to the group of men who were beginning to exit the church. Joshua's back was toward me as he followed the men. "Joshua," I spoke, fearing he would get away.

He turned to face me and I was stuck by the kindness in the eyes of this young man. "I know you?" he asked. "No," I replied, "but you're about to know me and something else I think will be of interest."

Not knowing what else to say, I raised the Bible to his view and pulled back the cover. "Do you recognize this?" I queried. Now as amazed as I was, it was obvious he, too, was mystified. His eyes met my gaze as he proffered, "That's my Bible. I haven't seen it in several years. How did you get it? Why do you have it?"

As he paged through the book as if discovering an old friend, I related the story of finding it in the dumpster, ending with, "And now I'd like to know the rest of the story from you."

Obviously dumbfounded he seemed to search his mind for answers to that and the other items I'd found. "Maybe I gave it to one of the men. I don't really know and I can't give you answers about the letter either. Oh my!" Joshua offered.

"Well, it's obviously yours and I'd like to return it to you," I said reluctantly as I offered him the book. My heart melted at his response, "No, you keep it. It is apparent that it has blessed you."

NEVER CEASE TO BE AMAZED

I never cease to be amazed at how even the small desires of your heart are heard by a loving Heavenly Father. It seemed like such a selfish wish, and I have so many other Bibles in all versions and sizes and covers. Yes, all my versions of Scripture "read quite well" and the message is the same, but I'm really fond of this particular Bible which had become the center of an unfolding adventure with a young man and a ministry that had been unknown to me before this very hour.

No human could have orchestrated this Bible adventure in progress now unfolding. What are the chances that Sybille and I would recover a Bible from a dumpster and three or four years later find its owner? But just think of all the events that were required to bring this reunion to fruition. Sybille and I found the Bible and belongings several years before I closed the store. This Bible was one of the few things that I kept from the store. It was a turnkey sale so everything relating to the boutique stayed with the new owner. I even sold my store name: Kay's Kloset.

Because I sold the store I was able to buy a retirement home in town. I had lived in the country most of my married life and never thought living in town would be a possibility that I would welcome. I vividly remember my husband and I struggling to find just the right property to become our refuge. The rock home we built on our eleven acres was hidden by oaks and cedar and couldn't be seen by neighbors or from the road. We loved the solitude under the oak canopy where our only frequent visitors were God's creatures. I remember questioning David, my husband, when we bought the property: was he really sure he wanted to drive forty-five minute both to and from work? His answer was firm: "It makes it worth the drive when you live in such a peaceful place."

However, since my husband's death the acreage and home in the woods near Georgetown had become increasingly difficult to manage. I'd been looking at this very cottage on a retirement circle in Georgetown for at least a year and a half.

I found the cottage quite at the direction of God. Leaving church one Sunday I prayed "God, if it's in Your plan that I move to town You'll have to show me where I'm going." About that time there appeared in my field of vision a sign by the side of the road announcing, "Home for Sale." "Why not?" I thought as I turned right and followed the signs. Coming around the last turn I arrived at the curb in front of the house which was to become my new home. A calm sense of knowing came over me and I became excited.

However, this, too, would be an act of God. His timeline is not exactly ours and we often complicate our lives with human decisions that make things seem impossible in human ways. The house was under contract to someone else and an offer I made was not accepted. Also, suffice to say my financial situation at that time was not acceptable to the financial institutions. My husband had passed away. With that I not only lost the love of my life, but gone was the income that kept us financially floating. This was coupled with a financially struggling business in a less than optimal economy.

Struggling and stressing became an ever minute way of life. I kept on keeping on continually praying "Okay God, whenever You're ready to step in and relieve this situation, I'm ready." Truth is that I don't think I really was ready to yield to God's direction. I kept saying, "Okay, God I've got it. I understand. Let me do this." Such a headstrong woman I am and such a patient, tolerant God Father we have. I am so thankful He is never more than a prayer away and always such a loving Father.

When the time was God's another amazing event unfolded. People are still amazed that the boutique sold when it probably was against human odds that it would happen the way it did. The new owner would have a challenge and I prayed too that she was walking in God's plan for her life. Yet, the relief from the stress of managing a business and its financial stress would be reason to praise God again and again.

After struggling with what to do now with my living situation, I again found myself praying for my Father's guidance. My son, Bryon, and his family had moved into my country home and it was imperative that I find a new place to call home. They would love and care for the property in a way David and I once had done. Bryon wanted me to build out there on the property and I tried to make that happen. But it just wasn't right.

One day I was in town with a friend and feeling especially lost and ungrounded. Prayer was my only relief. Again that feeling of God's directing hand took over and I was overwhelmed to drive by the little house I fell in love with a year ago.

Can you just imagine the amazement I felt when I once again rounded that corner and found a "For Sale" sign in the yard? WOW! It was then that God whispered in my ear and acknowledgment that He had plans for me to prosper me and not harm me. Jeremiah 29:11 tells us that God has plans to give us a hope and a future. I had further confirmation that this was the chosen place for me when I went inside. It was now listed with a different realtor who had restaged the house. There in the kitchen was a beautiful red glass cookie jar. On top of the jar perched a red cardinal. Ever since David died red cardinals had been mysteriously showing up at opportune moments of decision. I don't remember noticing any before. Real ones came to the door and other cardinal signs appeared as if to give confirmation. Our high school mascot was a cardinal and I have fond memories of David in his red cardinal football jacket. So, I took the cookie jar as a sign. I didn't hesitate and wrote the contract which was readily accepted for a much reduced price. Within a few weeks the house was mine and it began to feel like home. The cardinal cookie jar still proudly sits atop the refrigerator in my new kitchen. The precious "found Bible" also made the trip and found a new home on the table beside my favorite chair. I did tell you how precious that book had become to me, didn't I?

One more interesting little God detail is necessary in this story. Paul, my wonderful neighbor and new friend, moved into my new neighborhood a few months after I did. He had lived in Georgetown most of his life but our paths never crossed. It's not that big of a town and he had at one time been a business manager in the Chamber of Commerce of which I was a member.

Paul had been married for forty-six years and was now making his way as a single. After apartment living in a cracker box for a period of time he purchased the house right across the street from me. I met him and his sister one day after a storm had crossed our neighborhood. I was out in the front yard with my friends trying to find the grassy yard which was now buried beneath a forest of fallen braches. I was confined to a wheel chair at the time because of a leg injury. My home damage was minimal compared to Paul's and his neighbor, who had watched helplessly as their common fence was toppled by the strong wind.

I didn't really know this new neighbor but had a few hints about the character of this man. The first clue was the cross he placed in his yard along with an American flag. Then, I watched as he and a few friends and neighbors rebuilt his fence. The helpers changed from day to day, but Paul was always there toiling away. I regret that I didn't take them lemonade on the obviously hot summer day. I was physically challenged at that time so I couldn't offer any other assistance, and they were strangers to me.

I had recently broken four bones in my foot and recovered only to tear a tendon and rupture another. There are blessings in everything as I came to discover. Being a can do person I don't know that I would have ever slowed down and taken time to relax if I hadn't been injured. But finding time to enjoy being at home didn't include forgoing my new hobby. I built a ramp myself so I could get out to the backyard in my wheelchair and walker.

I had found a love and pleasure in being in my new back yard. I took special pride in being able to grow things for the first time. David always said that the only plants I wouldn't kill were silk or plastic. He was right. But I guess there is a season for everything. I found great pleasure in bringing my bare back yard to life under the canopy of trees. Pads of turf were laid in scotch board pattern while a shade tolerant variety was seeded under the trees. Beds were created and edged with rocks from my other acreage; a patio was created with concrete squares in areas that were deemed by me to be intolerant of grass. Plants were planted while others were trimmed. One particularly gangling sticker bush became my version of a huge bonsai tree on which I daily attached bread and treats for my birds and squirrels. Lounging under the expansive Bradford pear tree in the evening with my Kindle became a favorite event for me. God and I spent many hours out there under the stars conversing. I could again feel the closeness to God that I had experienced at my country refuge. Have you felt the "peace that passes understanding?"

The yard really was taking shape, but my podiatrist was quite ticked that I didn't seem to be able to quit working in my yard in spite of my injuries. In fact, she was most irritated to find dirt down in my cast when she removed it and it didn't seem to matter that I had been sitting while repotting plants. She assumed I was still digging beds with my tiller which was somewhat true. I promised to try to enjoy the garden and quit working on my projects for a time.

One day when I could walk again for short periods and with a cane I took an excursion to the local home and garden store. Of course, the garden center was a magnet and soon I was purchasing four huge bags of garden soil for my beds. That was doable since they were more than willing to load it for me. It wasn't until I was on the way home that I realized the magnitude of the problem I had just created. And so, the dirt rode around with me for several weeks before I figured out a way to get it to my back yard.

One afternoon I stopped at Paul's house. I was apprehensive to ask for help. I never was good at asking for help being a do-it-yourself gal, but I managed. Paul willingly agreed to come over and assist.

Later that afternoon, Paul came over to help and we had a nice, get acquainted visit before the work began. However, I wasn't the only one that was anxious to get acquainted with Paul. I had recently taken in a little black and white Shih Tzu who needed to find a new home. His owner could no longer keep him, so I accepted the challenge of finding him a new owner and home. However, that afternoon it was JD, the cunning and smart pint-sized ball of fluff that was busy selling himself to our guest. JD hopped right up in Paul's lap and tried his best to be the center of attention. All I said was, "He's looking for a home." After the chat we ventured into the yard to attack the dirty task at hand. Paul hefted the large bags of soil from car to back yard easily. JD kept pace with Paul's every step. A "doggy grin" spread across his little face. Long story short, by the end of the visit Paul had gone from definitely not interested in adopting a dog to agreeing to take him home on trial. Needless to say, JD won Paul's heart and became a new pal and constant companion.

BACK TO THE MOMENT. REWIND TO CRESTVIEW

Now, go back to the moment at Crestview Baptist Church when God had brought me face to face with the original owner of that Bible. I was there for a reason that was yet to be revealed. But I was so sure in my heart that this was truly a God divined moment. I had many questions for Joshua and the bond became apparent. He told Paul and me about Oak Ridge Disciple House in the few minutes we had together. Paul seemed just as excited as I was to be part of this unfolding story. Joshua invited us to come out to disciple house for "Testify Night" which was a weekly event every Thursday. As I was processing that it was twenty plus miles out in the country somewhere, I heard Paul tell Joshua, "We'll be there." I was pleased and amazed that my new friend would so quickly sign on for this "God journey."

Joshua told us that in two weeks the Crestview minister would be the speaker at the Thursday event at Oak Ridge and that was most interesting to us. It was reassuring that another bridge of familiarity was being built for us to this somewhat mysterious event. Paul anxiously followed Joshua out to his truck to retrieve a DVD of Joshua's own testimony and some Oak Ridge flyers. Our excitement and amazement still permeated the moment as Paul drove me home and we vowed to meet one day to view the Joshua DVD together.

In a few days hence Paul and I sat down to view the DVD that Joshua gave us of his testimony. There he was on the screen speaking to a group of believers about his life story. Those beautiful green eyes showed the pain and suffering of his past life of addiction. Joshua says, "It is my blessing to share my story with you. I am praying that by the power of the Holy Spirit, it will penetrate hearts and give hope and encouragement to this lost and dark world. I too was once deep in darkness but the light of Christ was able to penetrate that darkness and change my heart. Where there was once anger and hurt, by His saving grace, there now is love and compassion to reach the lost and lonely. The only question I have for you today is: ARE YOU READY?"

Joshua Harris is the founder and servant of Oak Ridge Disciple House which is a non-profit, faith based, Christian character-building program geared toward reaching men who are broken from drug and alcohol addictions.

According to Joshua, "The sole purpose of the Oak Ridge Disciple House is to provide men struggling with drug and alcohol addiction an opportunity to spend six months with God and other Christians learning that starting a relationship with Jesus Christ is the first and most important step in finding freedom from the bondage of drug and alcohol addictions.

Seeing the DVD had been enough stimulus for Paul and I that we knew we wanted to experience this firsthand and so we decided to go to Oak Ridge for Testify that very Thursday. Excited about our first trip to Oak Ridge, we called Joshua for directions. My hand scribbled the list of directions but my mind began to question the sanity of our venture. The "over the river and through the woods" type list of directions went on and on and ended with, "You know you're at the gate when the unmarked pavement suddenly has a yellow stripe down the middle. Paul and I stepped into this adventure with trusting anticipation that God was in charge and directing our way. We were not disappointed. With the "found" Bible and a basket of freshly baked brownies in tow, we were off. Paul plugged road numbers into his GPS which he fondly calls "Gypsy" and I retrieved the scribbled directions from my pocket. On and on we drove through the countryside and through a little town. Thirty miles always seems longer when you don't know exactly where you're going, so the sight of the road number indicating our turn was a welcome sight. Now the narrow paved road wound through rocky hills and valleys. We were in search of the yellow stripe down the middle of the road.

Suddenly, there it was. At first sight of the yellow stripe I think we both sighed as we gazed right to find the cattle guard gate that led down a very narrow, winding road. The road quickly disappeared from sight as it went between cedar trees and brambles. "We're here!" I said as Paul turned down the little path. The truth of that statement is that it was a bit premature. We bumped and rocked down the worn pavement filled with potholes. The edges of the worn away pavement was bordered by Texas barbed wire fences that stretched between posts roughly cut from tree limbs. The two-mile road seemed to go on and on forever with no end in sight. Any semblance of the damaged pavement disappeared as we drove over an even rougher caliche path with deep ruts from long ago rains. Then there were the bumps. Ridges of dirt whose intent was to deflect water running down the rocky hillside occurred frequently on the road. Clusters of cedar trees choking the oaks that had preceded them blocked vision for a time. Then, they cleared to reveal miles of rolling Texas hill country, both descending and ascending as they stretched to the horizon above. We passed a number of cozy, rustic homes tucked into the woods between sporadic gatherings of goats in rocky pastures. A dry creek ran along one side for a portion of the road. It came to mind that this truly was a "Road Less Traveled" but that is someone else's story. I can only imagine what must have gone through the future disciples' minds as they first traveled this road to a place they would learn to call God's refuge on the ridge. In fact, we would soon find out that the disciples commonly referred to it as "Damascus Road."

A large gateway with a huge wooden cross greeted us finally as we arrived. Around another curve, we caught sight of a large wooden home with expansive porches on the front and side. We parked among the other cars and made our way to the house. A number of men of different sizes, heights, and ages came rushing from the door and down the steps. They looked so excited and pleased to see us and they didn't even know us. It's just that kind of place where love abounds. We had no idea of what to expect and were surprised to be joined by numbers of guests each toting buckets, baskets, and trays of food which were spread on an expansive table. Dinner prepared, Joshua greeted everyone with a short, newsy report and led the prayer. Then the eating began. Each of us filled our plates beyond comfortable and went out the long porches to be seated with groups of disciples and friends. Paul and I sat at a table and were joined by "the boys" and friends until there were eight of us. It was like one big happy family supper I that I remember from childhood. And these were strangers joined only by one common thread . . . a love of Jesus.

The conversation let us get to know some of the disciples seated with us and they were extremely open about themselves. We joined in the chipper conversation. I had not said much before one of the disciples exclaimed, "You're the Bible lady!" Some looked puzzled, but I grinned, knowing Joshua must have shared the story of the Bible I now possessed. What a nice visit we had together. That was the night I became known to the disciples as "the Bible lady" and I begin to feel a real sense of kinship with these guys. God is so good at putting people together at the right time and place for the edification of both. To God be the glory!

It seems appropriate to add Mike's story at this juncture because this is the point at which he entered the story. You see, Mike was the disciple who sat with us at dinner that evening and made my "Bible lady" identity known. Our connection was set at that moment and we still see him several years later. Mike was shorter than most disciples and a bit stocky, but he was so cute. He had black hair, eyes like coal, and a grin that never left his face. His ordinary stance was with his hands in his pocket. We came to know Mike and his heart as time passed. Mike graduated from Oak Ridge and went back to being a greasy diesel mechanic. But even now he's always at Testify on Thursday. He has given a leg up to a number of graduates by providing them an opportunity to learn his craft and be employed. He has mentored many of the men. He has become a leader at his church and is a trained Stephen minister. Now he is in charge of the Transition House where he fosters the graduates' continued growth. He is the only disciple to ever serve on the board of directors of Oak Ridge.

After a delicious meal of a wide assortment of dishes and dessert we settled into chairs to begin worship. The house was filled with joyful noise and songs praising God. Then, a guest speaker gave his testimony about his struggle with cancer. God meets us wherever we are if we seek Him. His love of God was evident to all present through his inspiring testimony. We don't all face the same troubles and hardships but we do all have one God who loves us and desires a relationship with us on a personal level.

FRETTING FOR NAUGHT

Our minister, Dan, was to be the speaker at Testify the next Thursday. Dan is an incredible teacher of the Word and I never tire of listening to him. His messages are always meaningful. In fact, on two different occasions he has spoken about events that paralleled my experiences with Joshua's Bible. One was the story of Bill Gray's lost Bible which found a new home in the mission field being shared with believers there. I don't remember all the details, but I know it gave me confirmation that these things happen in God's world. Having Dan there would make the evening more special.

Paul and I arrived at Oak Ridge again after traversing the winding road that had been a topic of conversation the week prior. "What must those new men think the first time they travel this? Perhaps they wonder if they're going to the end of the earth!" he gestured. We arrived laden with food for the sharing table and a gift for Joshua. I was so blessed by the gift of his Bible to me and the connection we had made that I wanted to give him something as a token of my thanks.

I fretted all week about something appropriate to take. All the time it was right there within eyesight. There was a book that I had given to a friend of mine. I had heard the author, John Eldredge, speak on television and his words rang true that it would be a message that could help my friend grow in his personal life. When we parted company he returned it to me unopened. Because the book was written for a male audience, I didn't know quite what I would do with it. I pondered giving it to our youth minister but didn't get the gut feeling that was where I needed to give it. I passed it on a shelf in my home office one day that week and felt like it jumped at me, screaming, "Take me." So yes, that would do nicely as a gift for Joshua, especially since he was involved in a ministry for men. I sat and lovingly labored over a personal letter to Joshua inside the front cover. Feeling pleased with the selection I asked God to bless it to His highest good. And so He would . . .

The same welcoming atmosphere permeated the house as we entered. Paul carried the casserole and found a place for it. I sought out Joshua with my gift. Pulling him aside, I quickly told him how much his Bible meant to me and that I wanted to give him something in return. I held out the book as his eyes fell on the title, *Way of the Wild at Heart*. As pleased as he was, he seemed distracted, as he glanced around the room. He stammered a bit as his eyes lit up with an idea and he told me to follow him. Although confused by his reaction, his statement reassured me: "God's going to blow your mind again. Watch!"

I followed closely as Joshua approached a tall, dark-haired, young disciple. He introduced me to Logan and then addressed him personally. "Logan, you came to me yesterday telling me you'd just finished reading the book *Wild at Heart*. You wanted more of that message because it resonated with you. You asked me to get you the next book, right?" Logan nodded and seemed curious. Beginning to get chills again, I realized what was unfolding in God's plan. Joshua offered the book to Logan, saying, "Look what she brought you!" Logan teared up and so did I. It was just another one of those wonderful God moments that happen when you are still and listen for His guidance. Joshua grinned from ear to ear!

Fear grabbed me as I blurted out, "But there's a personal letter to you, Joshua, inside the cover of the book." My fear quieted as Joshua replied, "Just let him read it." And I agreed knowing that God was directing. "I'll bring another one for him but he can read yours for now." Oh how we try to solve all our small human dilemmas!

But I did just that by going to the Christian store and buying another one before the next Testify. This time it would be for Logan to keep and Joshua could keep his copy with my letter. Money isn't as available to me now in retirement but I just knew it was something I had to do. So I acted only to find God's blessing in that too. At the book store I found a copy of the book that had just been put on the sale rack for five dollars. That made the deal even sweeter. And again I thanked my Heavenly Father.

Logan, Paul, and I developed a friendship and enjoyed many visits at the Ridge. One night Logan's mother came to me and introduced herself, thanking me for the book that I had given to Logan, and my kindness towards him. Long story short, we have become good friends and enjoyed many visits together. Mothers of these men have a special burden to bear that only a mother's heart can understand. I have been so blessed by her testimony. She's very proud of her son and rightly so. But it's difficult not to be consumed with fear when you know what they face when they re-enter the real world and are around others who may have influenced their problems. What does one say when you hear that one of Logan's influencers in the drug world would still be in his life? My mind has often wandered to the plight of these guys returning to family and friends who were part of the problem. Sometimes they can't just invent a new life with all new people. In fact, that is almost always impossible. As much as I am impressed by the work of this program in turning lives over to Jesus and becoming a new man, I am filled with need to pray for those returning to the world after graduation. That thought could be foreboding if God were not involved. God willingly goes with these men as they leave and desires nothing more than to be their greatest source of strength. The mountains of life are high and the valleys are deep but our God is faithful to the end if we allow Him to guide and protect. We all face a multitude of troubles and live in a garden of temptation in the real world. What's important? Keep your eyes upon Jesus!

What happened to Logan? He buried his "old man," his former life, as over seventy others have done in the Oak Ridge cemetery. He reentered real life and as far as we know lives as a new man in Christ. We used to see him once in a while in the dairy department of our supermarket. But according to social media he now works nights so we don't get to touch base personally. We still pray for him and the others who have graduated.

One by one the men became more familiar to us. Putting names and stories with each one became a challenge to Paul and me as we continued our treks to the Ridge. Paul seemed to identify with one disciple easily, perhaps because they shared the same first name. My friend Paul and Disciple Paul found a common ground to chat in spite of their diverse backgrounds. Disciple Paul stood out from the others perhaps because he took center stage at worship time. Accompanied by Logan on the drum box he would play his guitar and sing worship songs as we gathered together. What a beautiful faith and love of Jesus he displayed; the joy was written on his face as he sang. The group sang praises but above the crowd was evident the bold voices of the disciples praising God for transformation and guidance in their new lives. We were overjoyed and sad when graduation time came for Disciple Paul. Some of those sad feelings dissipated over the next few visits as we saw other disciples step up to lead the worship. One frequent visitor even commented on how amazing it was that God always seemed to have someone in the wings to lead the worship as men cycled in and out of the center.

Paul gave his testimony one Thursday shortly before his graduation and we also attended his Sunday afternoon graduation. His story had similarities to the others with destruction of lives through drugs and alcohol. His climb out of the pit had not been easily accomplished with at least one relapse. But now he made it to the brink of a new life guided by Heavenly Father. He would soon return to his home in West Texas. His son, the love of his life, attended the graduation with other family and proudly mounted the stage to hug his dad. Paul had talked many times about how much he loved the boy and wanted to be in his life. Now that path was available. Praise God! Yes, I still see Paul on

Facebook occasionally and hear about him from other guys in that group.

Another father who was a single father comes to mind, too. His name was David. He was in discipleship several years later than Paul. He was a gentle soul who seemed to have little to say, but always a willing worker. His ways were admirable and he hid his pain well. His son lives in a town not many miles from here. The boy lives with his mother. Even after graduation, David rarely got to see his son. When he did it was in a highly supervised situation. Yes, he'd earned the punishment. Now he has realized what his foolish choices have cost him and is trying to become worthy of more trust. David lived in the Transition House for a time, and is gainfully employed. He now has a place of his own and is working on being a better father to his son.

This story reminds me of another disciple who came to the Ridge a year or so after Paul graduated. His name was Frank and his picture and story on Facebook brought to mind how much children need and deserve a good father. Children too can be part of God's plan in reaching the lost father. Joshua posted a request for prayer for Frank the day he came to the "round table" at the Ridge. The "round table" is a discussion that takes place the first day a new disciple arrives at the Ridge. The candidate is able to share their story with the Oak Ridge staff and then given the opportunity to commit to the program. Frank was not unlike the others who come to Oak Ridge to find God and new life. His little red headed daughter had discovered him unconscious on the kitchen floor and called for help. A child and God led him to open the door to a new life. That really spoke to my heart. Frank and his little girl were a family of two. Sometimes someone would bring her to Testify to see her dad. The smiles each of them wore on those occasions was evidence of a loving bond. When Frank told his story at Testify, his little girl listened attentively to her daddy's story as tears rolled down her cheeks. They were good tears of releasing pain and experiencing joy. Frank changed so much during his discipleship, one could hardly believe it was the same man. After graduation, Frank and his daughter moved fairly close to our town. This enables him to have contact with his Oak Ridge brothers. I see them in church and at the Ridge quite often. The bouncy, curly-haired, happy girl is almost always right beside her daddy. The grin on her face shows the pride and love she holds. I could play the "What If" game and think of what might have happened to this family, but most important is the outcome through the grace extended by a loving Heavenly Father.

DAY IN THE LIFE. SERVANT'S HEART

*J*oshua keeps these guys busy and every moment filled so there is no room to slip. It gives new meaning to togetherness when you think about how the program is constructed. There are twelve beds for twelve disciples. The staff members stay on site and are never far away. Each man gradually earns privileges as he meets the expectations of the program. Joshua knows them well but he knows addiction and its traps even better, so every effort is made to insure individual success.

Morning comes early as they roll out of bed to attend worship and study in the Ridge Chapel. Can't you just hear twelve plus guys' voices praising God at 4:30 AM? I would bet that's a new experience for them. And, it's not the only new experience. Their days are filled with learning opportunities, group work and teaching. Memorizing scripture is an important part of the program. That's a good example for all to follow. Keep the word of God tucked in your heart and mind where it is always accessible. Several times Paul and I have had the pleasure of hearing them recite as a group:

"Finally, be strong in the Lord and in His mighty power. Put on the full armor of God so that you can take your stand against the devil's schemes. For our struggle is not against flesh and blood, but against the rulers, against the authorities, against the powers of this dark world and against the spiritual forces of evil in the heavenly realms. Therefore, put on the full armor of God, so that when the day of evil comes, you may be able to stand your ground, and after you have done everything, to stand. Stand firm then, with the belt of truth buckled around your waist, with the breastplate of righteousness in place, and with your feet fitted with the readiness that comes from the gospel of peace. In addition to all this, take up the shield of faith, with which you can extinguish all the flaming arrows of the evil one. Take the helmet of salvation and the sword of the Spirit, which is the word of God. And pray in the Spirit on all occasions with all kinds of prayers and requests. With this in mind, be alert and always keep on praying for all the saints." Ephesians 6:10–18

Several evenings a week other Christian men and leaders come to teach them. On Tuesday nights they attend Celebrate Recovery, on Wednesday they attend evening worship, and Thursday is always Testify on the mountain. There is also time scheduled for property maintenance work, housekeeping, laundry and all the activities. And that's not all!

Joshua has a big servant's heart. He wants the disciples to develop a love of helping others also. So, he schedules them for all kinds of service projects. They spend a lot of time helping maintain the property at First Baptist Church and for individuals.

One of the things I admire most is the teamwork in moving people. Yes, moving people from house to house. Diane and Ernie, our friends who had first directed our attention the disciples at Crestview. When Diane and Ernie moved to Dallas-Fort Worth, the guys were there to help. Can you just imagine twelve guys showing up to load the truck? Their respectful attitudes are on display as they work together. They glorify good being willing helpers of those in need and expect nothing in return.

Chester, a former disciple and current staff member, was in charge. Diane and Ernie had planned for the arrival of the Oak Ridge guys and the rented truck was already in the driveway. They had spent hours packing boxes and labeling. The team, at Chester's direction, moved to load the truck and were done within a couple hours. I got to watch it firsthand since I went to pick up two chairs and an entertainment center from Diane and Ernie. The guys even loaded me up and one disciple went with my son and me to unload. I was entrusted with this disciple's care for a short time after Chester gave me instructions. By the time we returned the disciples were through and ready to leave. It certainly took a big load off my friends and allowed them to get on with moving. Diane and Ernie returned in a couple of days to tie up loose ends and to close on the sale of the house. A pleasant surprise awaited them. The disciples had gone back and cleaned the house from top to bottom without being asked. What a blessing they are learning to become at Oak Ridge. "For we do not preach ourselves, but Jesus Christ as Lord, and ourselves as your servants for Jesus' sake." 2 Corinthians 4:5

Only recently was I privileged to receive an assistance project from the disciples. Although it happened much later than the previous example it reveals another service gifted by the disciples. As spring approached my whole yard was in dire need of attention. Although I still love to work in my yard, it has become more of a challenge as years pass. Things like relocating shrubbery, trimming trees, and cleaning gutters are not advisable. It became overwhelming for me. So, I asked Chester if they could come one day and do a spring rejuvenation project for my yard and Paul's yard. He agreed and the day was scheduled. The guys seemed anxious to come.

I think they were excited that we planned a meal for them when the work was done. The van and trailer pulled up in front of the house shortly before nine. The van doors flew open and out jumped the disciples. They grabbed yard tools; some of them went to Paul's house to begin work, some stayed with at my house. I communicated my list of tasks to the staff and off they all went. My job was to go around the front and back yards to give further directions and answer questions. They kept me hopping as they quickly moved from this task to that. Each of them was occupied with digging up plants to replant, trimming trees and bushes, cleaning gutters, getting rid of dead plants and empty pots, creating borders on beds, mulching, weeding, and whatever else needed to be done.

John became my tree trimmer and did a great job. It wasn't an easy task, but he seemed to enjoy it. John was excited about his upcoming completion of the program and going home to his wife-to-be and two children. "We'll be back to see you, Mama Kay. It's not that far away. We're going to stay in touch." We attended his wedding and have kept in touch. It's not easy, but God is there for them.

One of the disciples found a birdhouse and mounted it in a tree while others attached trellis for my climbing rose. It took three of them and several opinion givers to mount the sign from my former store to my wooden fence. "Let's make it light up so they'll know its Kay's garden," hollered one fellow, while another suggested that it would be simpler just to add twinkle lights. It gives a nice touch to the yard between the new flower bed with climbing jasmine and the yellow climbing rose by the purple blooming mountain laurel. My fountain was cleaned out and put into operation. "That's a calming sound," said one disciple, completing the task. "Yes," I replied, "this is where I spend time with God in the calm, cool of evening. The sound of water makes it even more peaceful. The overhanging canopy of trees gives shade by day, but the stars are my canopy at night. God and I have had quite a few chats out here." He just smiled while another fellow nodded in agreement. One of the youngest disciples took it upon himself to spread ant poison on ant mounds that had appeared along the fence and flower beds. He was so hyper that it kept him busy constructively instead of catching my geckos. It looked like hide and seek to me, but he seemed to have fun. It was a frenzy of activity for several hours and it made my heart sing. As work wound down, it was obviously time to eat. Paul came over with freshly baked beans. I got the pulled pork ready to serve onto buns with an assortment of condiments. Other friends brought barbecue chicken for sandwiches, also. Spoons were placed in the coleslaw and potato salad; drinks were chilled in a tub of ice. We joined together in offering a prayer of thanksgiving. It was my pleasure being with the guys and serving them too. They excitedly filled their plates and went out to the backyard to find a place to settle in and eat. Joshua even came and had dinner with us. Small clusters of disciples and friends lounged while eating and chatting. I chose a recliner close to Joshua and a few others. It was good to talk with him about plans for the program. "Serve wholeheartedly, as if you were serving the Lord, not men." Ephesians 6:7

ALL WORK AND NO PLAY?

*I*t may sound like all of the disciples' time is spent worshipping, learning, or serving. However, they manage to find time for play, too. Joshua always is a good role model when it comes to physical fitness expectations. After all, our bodies are the temple of God and we invite Jesus into our hearts. If Jesus were coming to your house, you would make an effort to see that it was fit for him. Our bodies become a living sacrifice. Now I think I've gone to preaching instead of sharing a story. So, let's explore what the disciple do to accomplish this.

First of all, being on the property surrounding the Ridge is like a campground with scenic views and nature trails up and down the rugged terrain. There is a gym and a small pool on site, plus expansive areas for games of all sorts. Obviously, the playground equipment is for the children of the disciples and visitors. I'm sure most of this was all developed as a result of gifts from supporters and hard physical labor of disciples in residence. We sometimes see disciples hitting golf balls or tossing Frisbees in the open area when we go out on Thursday evening. Families gather at the swings nearby and laughter fills the air as quality time is spent with loved ones. Occasionally there will be several guys sitting on benches under the broad oak trees. Time is spent visiting there while playing board games or cards. I was even a little surprised to see some of them playing chess. Chess is a game I respect, but never played. You have to be blessed with strategical thinking to play.

Gatherings are currently held on the deck surrounding the main house. We've spread out a great deal since we first began going. Tables now go around the three sides of the house for the meal. After eating, the boys quickly assemble rows of chairs for worship and the testimony on the main part of the deck. At times there is overflow from the deck into the yard. One night recently, lots and lots of people came when the new minister at First Baptist came to share his testimony. Seating was moved out into the driveway for the crowd and he spoke from the deck. It's always so inspiring to witness so many Christians gather in community to worship.

Rumor has it there may be plans for a pavilion to be built to accommodate larger crowds and provide shelter from inclement weather events. Two men from the community are currently making plans for this structure which may even include barbecue facilities. One of the men has gone to the Ridge with us and the ministry really spoke to his heart. The other, a friend of the first, knows the property well and even helped construct part of the main house years ago. Well, they're drawing plans, brainstorming ideas, and gathering material estimates to present to Joshua. Of course, Joshua would have to approve any building. Once he did approve it, they would secure donations to fund it. Getting the money doesn't seem to concern them. One of them said, "If God is in this and it's His plan, the money will be there." That's a supreme example of faith in action and servant hearts.

Other supporters enjoy time with the disciples where they can share their talents and help develop skills. And, the disciples are from such varied backgrounds that there is a great deal of talent and skill to share with brothers, too. Some are book smart with college degrees while others have developed amazing skills in mechanic or building trades.

At a later point I will share with you the story of a disciple that could not read. When I shared it with a disciple's mother, she had more to tell me about the disciple's learning. Emily and Doyle became acquainted with the ministry about the same time Paul and I did. Doyle tells of their first adventure to the Ridge for Testify. He asked Emily what she thought about the experience on the way home. "We're coming back!" she replied. And they certainly have come back. They saw a need for some of the guys to develop better reading skills and pass a GED so they would be more employable in the real world. Patiently, they have assumed this task and spend many hours tutoring these boys and building confidence. The disciple's mom went on to explain how difficult it had been in school for her son and he ended up not graduating. He needed a GED to even be considered for a job. He had the ability, but had missed the opportunity until Emily and Doyle took him under their wing to coach. He succeeded and got his GED and was able to secure a job after graduation.

Doyle has another talent, too. He's a magician. But, not just a magician; he's a Christian magician. I stared with great interest as he wove the story of salvation into his magic tricks with cards and scarves of many colors.

There are numbers of supporters from First Baptist, the home church of the disciples. Some of them lead groups while others play musical instruments for Bible class and Testify worship. Others are mentioned elsewhere but there are far too many to name individually.

One couple cannot go without mention. John and Debbie serve on the board of directors. It doesn't stop there. They've offered lodging to families of disciples who are visiting and most recently hosted a wedding at their home for another family closely involved with the Ridge. Every fall Debbie buys a group of tickets for Spirit Fest in Round Rock. We buy tickets from her so we can all be together with the disciples. The Sunday afternoon music and praise festival is enjoyed by all.

Twice a year on the Fourth of July and Memorial Day, Debbie and John host a picnic in their own backyard for the disciples and supporters. The pool is made ready. Volleyball courts and ping pong tables are set up. Tents, tables, and chairs are all put in place. The hosts supply fried chicken and guests all arrive with lots and lots of delectable morsels. There are chips and dips, fresh vegetables, watermelon, and other fruits. I always try to take melon and corn on the cob drenched in butter. Joshua addressed me with butter oozing down his face: "Mama Kay, you think you got enough butter on that corn? It sure is good." It's an afternoon well spent with fun and frolic for all.

SEASON OF HOPE

Fall quickly passed and we were on to winter. Seasonal change isn't very evident in central Texas. If it weren't for Christmas decorations going up all over town, you'd hardly notice. Posters appeared announcing special events of the Christmas season and calendars were soon filled with lots of opportunities to celebrate Christmas. Georgetown is a unique and beautiful town in which to be during this season.

Our downtown square around the county court house is as vibrant and old fashioned as one can imagine. The old Chisholm Trail once went through the town built over 100 years ago. Statues of three legged Willie, a city founder, and Mr. Gold, a department store proprietor guard the square. Coffee houses, unique restaurants, candy stores and wineries offer a variety of eats to guests walking the square. People enjoy visiting the variety of stores on the square; there are boutiques, jewelry stores, toy stores, music stores, antique shops, handcraft stores, gift shops and others. The square is such a pleasant place to spend time.

People flock to the square during the Christmas season to enjoy all it has to offer as well as beautiful decorations. It becomes very magical with white lights outlining buildings and blossoming in the many trees. Everyone especially looks forward to the first weekend in December known fondly as "The Christmas Stroll." Vendors of unique items fill the streets. Kids' play areas and a "Bethlehem Town" entertain the huge crowds. Music is everywhere from several entertainment stages.

There's a holiday parade that is well attended on Saturday morning. Naturally, music fills the air as floats decked out for Christmas pass in review. I know one time I was pleasantly surprised to see the Oak Ridge disciples on a float depicting the disciples with Jesus. Who else would you cast as disciples? They were awesome. Now my memory sometimes fails me and I can't be certain they were in the holiday parade or the spring parade, but I do know for certain that I saw them on a float in a parade. At one event, the disciples had a booth to pass out information on salvation to the passersby. I came upon them and enjoyed visiting with them until I discovered my keys were missing. "Oh, no," I exclaimed, "I think I locked my keys in the car." Disciples looked at me with concerned. I heard one of them say, "Take this guy. He used to break in cars. He'll help you!" Laughter erupted. Fortunately, I didn't have a disciple return to criminal acts as my son came to save the day with extra keys. Thank goodness for cell phones.

The real reason for the season is Jesus and due to this, many church events are scheduled. One of the most special Christmas events for me is a holiday ladies' brunch held at First Baptist Church. Groups of women each decorate a table with a holiday theme. Of course, there's a spirit of competition so the displays become very elaborate and beautiful. I was privileged to attend and be seated at one of several tables done by a former disciple's wife, Audrey. Her husband, Tolbert, was one of the very first disciples at Oak Ridge and he now teaches there at least once a week. The theme for the year was books about Christmas. Each of the fifty tables displayed a different book with coverings, trimming, elaborate centerpieces, favors, place settings of china, and some even had lights or candles. The disciples didn't miss an opportunity to serve. Current disciples and graduates exited the kitchen with huge trays laden with scrumptious food prepared by the local restaurant, Laurie's Too. Each man had been assigned to a certain table and dressed according to the theme of the book at that table. There were angels and elves, snowmen and soldiers, truckers and little boys among the fifty men who helped. And Joshua? Well, what else would you expect? He was a wise man.

Christmas is family time at home with those you love. It's a time when family ties are pulled tighter and our minds revel in memories of Christmas passed. It's a happy time, at least it was as I grew up. My parents and I always attended Christmas Eve service at church. Christmas Day was complete with big dinners with extended family and gift exchanges. Women scurried about the kitchen while the men sat and whittled while they chatted on the front porch. My cousins and I would romp and play with our new treasured toys. I had a rude awakening over years of adulthood; I learned that it's not a picture perfect Norman Rockwell Christmas for everyone. It was only later in life that I became aware of just how painful and sad Christmas is for some people. Life goes on even though Christmas happens.

And so it did out on the Ridge. You don't just stop the program because it's Christmas. The guys are still there. They get up at four every morning to start their day with praise and worship. Then, they follow a busy schedule of service projects, study, chores, and more. Depending on where they are in their individual programs, they may or may not have contact with their families. Again, some have destroyed any relationships they had while in the grasp of addiction.

The beauty is that because they are accepting Jesus as Lord of their lives and learning about him every day these guys discover the true joy and meaning of Christmas without the trappings of man contrived additions to the holiday. At the Ridge a Christmas meal is shared with the guys as people show up laden with goodies and side dishes. Someone usually prepares turkey or ham. Audrey usually directs the preparation and presentation. What a talent for event planning and direction she has! Again, she is the wife of one of the very first disciples and they are still very committed to the program.

Yes, there are gifts. Usually disciples are given items they really need for personal care, dress, or edification. That's a lot of gifts to come up with and my budget is limited. I wanted so badly to give each one something personal, but I need to use restraint in my money department. So, I took tiny little foil wrapped gift boxes and inserted a Bible verse that I selected for each disciple. I gave them to a staff member to share with the men at an appropriate time. It took me years to really understand that it is more blessed to give than to receive. It wasn't much but it was a "warm fuzzy" for me and hopefully blessed them, too.

THE SURPRISE LISTENER

Paul and I love going to the Ridge for Testify; we continued going most every Thursday. Each evening is heartwarming, but I'd like to share one very unique evening. The events of the evening were in God's hands and it was so exciting to be part of it. But little did we expect anything like the story that unfolded. Near the end of the evening a new face, a new disciple approached me. "I'm Diane and Ernie's son-in-law," he said as he approached me. My face must have revealed my puzzled thoughts. "That was my story you just shared," he clarified. He was Greg. Greg was the family member of Diane and Ernie, the couple who had opened the next chapter in my life by telling Paul and me about Oak Ridge and Joshua at Crestview Baptist Church some time before. Apparently he had fallen but was back at the source of becoming whole on the ridge.

The Surprise Listener

My hug was welcomed by Greg as I realized that a name in my story now had a face. "Oh my, I am so glad to meet you. Diane and Ernie couldn't say enough about your journey through Oak Ridge and how proud they are of you." I heard myself say. Yet, my mind was racing quickly reviewing the story I had just shared with the group. Did I tell it right? Did I in any way offend the person I'd just spoken of to the group? And, by the way what was he doing here? I thought he was in Lubbock.

Earlier in the evening we had socialized with the group of visitors and enjoyed a meal with the disciples. Greg and another new arrival at Oakridge had joined the table of other disciples, Paul, and I as we ate and chatted. I was totally unaware of the connection we had at that time.

Later in the evening we gathered in the group room. Disciples speedily converted the meal setting to a room full of chairs quickly filled by guests, families, and disciples who awaited the testimony to come. I had left "the Bible" on a coffee table which needed to be moved to accommodate chairs for the large group. I claimed "the Bible" as someone raised it and tried to find its owner. I was sharing the quick version of "the Bible story" with a lady seated next to me who held a little girl in her lap. As I turned to the cover of "the Bible" to reveal Joshua's name, the child with beautiful brown eyes and hair reached for the book. "That's my daddy's Bible," she said, "I'll take it to him." Jumping down to the floor she reached for the book and scurried off to place it in Joshua's hands. "Daddy, she found your Bible," she announced. Joshua looked at me and questioned if this was "IT." I nodded and he smiled saying that he'd like to use it and share the story with the group. "You don't mind, do you?" he asked. And so, with my nod of approval he began the evening event with the story.

Joshua read from the Bible and noted underlining and notes he'd added years before. I had added my own notes and underlining. He seemed to approve as he became reacquainted with his old Bible.

Joshua selected and shared a reading of scripture for the evening. Then, he began the story of the Bible lady and asked me to clarify some of the events, but quickly turned the floor over to me to tell. I told the story to the best of my recollection. We even got a few laughs when we told how I'd found the letter with the Bible and other belongings that told of the end of a young man's life who had been troubled with drug addiction. That led me to deduce that a young man had died and these must have been his belongings discarded by family or friends in a dumpster. Joshua added that the letter probably was his own letter of submission when he ended his old ways and became renewed and alive

The Surprise Listener

in Jesus. "I wasn't really dead," he laughed, "but like the other disciples we bury our old man, our previous lives when we become new creatures in Christ."

No, he wasn't dead, but very much alive as a new man. And, here I stood, in response to a call from God to follow. He had been a LOSER who became a WINNER. I had FOUND and was so blessed to KEEP what I had was in that dumpster. It had opened the next chapter in my life and it led me with God's direction to an infinite number of men who have become my sons by adoption. Oh, I didn't legally adopt these guys, but they do hold a special place in this mother's heart. I shared with them a little bit about my own adoption and my son's tragic death. I made some comment about Abraham and Isaac and God's promise that his children would be as numerous as stars in the sky. Time seemed to stand still and I can still see that broad smile and glowing eyes of Joshua as he looked at me and said, "You can be my mama." Some of our closest family members do not share the same blood but a connection in the heart. That was the day he first called me Mama Kay.

I went on with the story telling how after several years I had come to the amazing story of Oak Ridge Disciple House and the realization that Joshua was alive and well and serving God at Oak Ridge. Diane and Ernie had so passionately shared their family member's story and the Oak Ridge story. They had unknowingly opened the door to the rest of the story. But then, that is how God works opening each new chapter one step at a time when we least expect it. I never cease to be amazed at how God brings the right people, who may have been strangers, together at just the right moment to guide and direct our pathways to walk in His way and fulfill His kingdom on earth.

"In all your ways acknowledge Him, and He will make your paths straight." Proverbs 3:6

Some weeks later, Joshua shared a story about his oldest daughter. She and her boyfriend had been involved in a horrible automobile accident with a huge truck. They were rammed into a nearby power pole. Amazingly, they not only survived, but were virtually unhurt. Stories like this pull at my heart strings because of my son's fatal crash. It's most horrible and painful to suffer that loss, but I can rejoice that God spared these two young people from harm. Cody, my son, had been out of high school as a graduate for two weeks and it was two more weeks before his birthday that his accident happened. A fiery crash of a car in which he was a passenger claimed his life. Again, an event shook me to my core emotionally when my granddaughter, who had just graduated, wrecked her mother's car because she made a bad choice. She, too, was unscathed though the car was totaled. It was just another reminder to me that we are responsible for the choices we make in life. Some of them may be tragic.

A third event involving a young man who was Cody's age at the time of his death occurred on the same section of highway as Cody's accident gave me more reason to process my thoughts. This young man, a family friend, was on his way to work at the super market when it happened. Cody had worked for the same super market. Wow! I really saw the similarities. However, this young man, Josh, survived the accident only to be in hospitals and rehabs for more than a year. Small progress like being able to turn his head on his own are still celebrated. Oh, the pain this family feels. I don't know that I would have handled their situation with the faith they have, but others have remarked that they don't know how I survived our event with the faith I displayed. It's just about knowing God as your best friend and companion.

I've had lots of time to think about all of these events as they pertain to my faith. I don't know why choices were made or why the outcome for each event was different. But I do know that God never gives us more than we can bear. And, if we truly seek Him, He will give us peace.

The disciples at Oak Ridge have choices, too. They haven't made good choices in their past or they wouldn't be there. There's lots of pain in their lives too. Prayers need to be invoked for each of them as well as our own families that God will guide them. We pray that they will make good choices and walk with God though the road is rough.

"The Lord is righteous in all His ways and loving toward all He has made. The Lord is near to all who call on Him, to all who call on Him in truth." Psalm 145:17–18

"No temptation has seized you except what is common to man. And God is faithful; He will not let you be tempted beyond what you can bear. But when you are tempted, He will also provide a way out so that you can stand up under it." 1 Corinthians 10:13

FAMILY OF GOD

"And how from infancy you have known the Holy Scriptures, which are able to make you wise for salvation through faith in Christ Jesus." 2 Timothy 3:15

Never did I question my relationship with God, my Father; or Jesus, my Savior; or Holy Spirit, my Guide. But more often than not I found myself struggling with my place in the body of Christ, my church. Being Lutheran was just the way I was supposed to be. It was the church of my mother's whole family. I went to Lutheran school from kindergarten through eighth grade. Every Sunday my father drove me to Sunday school while my mother put on the traditional Sunday dinner after which they joined me in church.

Upon graduation I received a scholarship to Concordia Lutheran College. I was totally convinced of my call as a Christian teacher however, that education was cut short because of a decision I made. I was very much in love with a young man from Oklahoma. At Christmas I accepted an engagement ring and we promised to marry after we graduated. Unfortunately, our plans were not acceptable to the college and church. This was still back in the day when the church couldn't believe that a young woman could serve the church and become married. I chose to give up my scholarship and education at Concordia. I never did understand the conflict and apparently neither did God. Don't you love it when God smiles? You see, I am the only one of six of my Concordia friends who taught in a Lutheran School. And though I never married the young man, he later became a Lutheran minister. Man cannot foil God's plan.

Well, this is important to my story only because it was the first of many things that created doubt about my church. Later, as a Lutheran teacher, I attended a Lutheran conference and became totally distressed. One of the leaders had expounded on his belief that a wife would not be saved if her husband wasn't saved. Whoa! My relationship with God was personal and my salvation was not dependent upon my husband's salvation. Yep, I was unequally yoked. But I prayed for my husband and believed God would touch his heart. He did believe and accept Christ but it took forty years to get to that point. This is just another example how God doesn't operate on our timeline, but He is faithful, just, and desires all men to be saved.

Without making this my autobiography let me fast forward to recent times. During the years I'd tried other churches including the full gospel movement. I became keenly aware of the importance of being well versed in scripture and not accepting every teaching as truth. When we moved to Georgetown I returned to the Lutheran church. The services were not as formal as my precious church. I loved my minister and church in Georgetown, but something was missing. My experience was worshipful and edifying. However, there was no sense of community outside the walls of the church. I tried attending Bible class and helping with events. I even joined several boards and organizations. But there was still a big hole in my heart for community. Everyone knew me and were welcoming inside church and activities, but it stopped at the church door with few exceptions.

Paul attended the Lutheran church with me several times, but it was quickly evident that we were both more at home at the Baptist church. The Bible teaching was sound and the community was incredible. Members became friends who were interested in my life inside and outside the church. I found myself looking forward to church three times a week and Bible studies and fellowship. It was a pleasure and not a duty.

Yet, I struggled on several levels. I really wanted to be part of this church. One of the most difficult for me was the Baptist belief in baptism by immersion to join the church. I felt challenged. God had obviously been my guide and loved me enough to want me to be his own. Events in my life were evidence of this. So, why did I have to be immersed to become a member? Wasn't my sprinkling good enough? At one time, I'd even been immersed in a Christian church but had no records. I didn't speak with anyone at church about my deep feelings or struggle. I certainly didn't discuss this with church friends or Paul. I had a fear that Paul would not take my conversion well. I certainly didn't want him to think I had ulterior motives about forwarding our relationship. I prayed and prayed for God's will for me and for Him to let me feel in my heart what to do.

The answer came and it was so reassuring. Again the answer came from a source I least expected. I realized by the calm that overcame my spirit when it happened that becoming a Baptist was part of God's plan for me. An Oak Ridge disciple provided the witness and the assurance I needed.

On Sunday mornings I had been attending Life Class at First Baptist where Joshua Harris was the teacher. Later, I would join Paul and our friends at Crestview for worship and lunch. Early mornings were spent with my family of disciples from Oak Ridge and their friends and families. The dawning of my understanding occurred at this class. Gregg was nearing graduation. He was Diane and Ernie's son-in-law. Joshua talked about Gregg and his faith. Then, he explained that Gregg had asked to be baptized to recommit his life to Jesus. He explained that Gregg had been baptized before but he felt compelled by free will to take this step again to publicly profess his faith. It was as if God pulled a light switch in my mind. It was more than okay. It was good to publicly rededicate your life to Christ with a humble heart.

My heart leaped for joy and I was assured of my path. After class I talked with Joshua about my decision to be baptized and join the Baptist church. Being baptized by Joshua on the same Sunday as Gregg was significant to me. God had led me to these disciples and Joshua and the Baptist church. I told Joshua that I would like to become a member of Crestview but would like to be baptized with Gregg. Without his family witnessing about Oak Ridge, without Paul introducing me to Sunday evenings at Crestview, and without Joshua Harris's Bible I would not have come to this moment of profession of faith. God truly had a plan for my life that I couldn't have imagined. I was excited and thrilled at my recommitment to Jesus.

It would be a week! And, now I had to share the news with Paul. I was filled with apprehension as I didn't want Paul to misunderstand my intention. My intent was really pure love for God and commitment to faith. I had to tell him of my upcoming baptism with Joshua and my intent to join Crestview. I talked it over with a good friend on earth and one in Heaven. And, I rehearsed how I would say what I needed to share.

The afternoon visit came and I prayed quietly for my friend and for me. I really was fearful of losing my friend, but my fears weren't realized. He truly is my best friend. A smile crossed his face as I spoke and I knew he was celebrating with me. Somehow that man reads my real heart like a book and loves me in spite of myself. He truly is a fine Christian who lives his faith.

My relief was short-lived. Fear set in as I begin to wonder what my son would think. I had raised him in the Lutheran church and Christian faith. It was the one thread that somehow held our relationship together. Christmas and holidays at church were special to both of us and I treasured the time we worshipped together. One afternoon he came to visit me after work. "Mom," he announced, "I want to go to church with you Sunday. It's Mother's Day." Oh my goodness! I had decided to tell him after the event because I was fearful of his approval. God is really working with me on my need to find human approval and my fear of rejection. This would be the first Mother's Day since my youngest son's death that I wasn't filled with dread. Mother's

Day was to be the day of my baptism at the Baptist church. There was no way out. I had to tell him.

"Son, I'd love to go to church together but we're going to have to change some things." I explained about my decision to join the Baptist church and be baptized on Sunday. "I confess I was reluctant to tell you, but I'd love to share the day with you," I stated. I carefully explained my decision and looked to him for a reaction. He just looked at me lovingly and said, "I'm not surprised." After talking for a bit we agreed to meet together on Mother's Day at the Baptist church. I was thrilled he would go and be with me. Paul couldn't attend because he drives the pick-up cart at church on Sunday. I hadn't told anyone else besides the disciples.

Sunday came and I walked with Joshua and Gregg to the back entrance of the church. Joshua quickly explained what to expect and what to do. Then, I was led to a room to change as church began. Gregg was first and then it was my turn. I was excited and very sure of my decision. I confessed Jesus as my Savior and was immersed while supported by Joshua's strong arms. I'm still amazed at how God brought us to that point. I stood and raised my arms to praise God and it was done.

After dressing I entered the sanctuary and located my son. He was sitting near the back of the sanctuary several rows behind the disciples. Bryon whispered to me saying, "When you came down to the water they invited all your friends and family to stand. I thought I'd be the only one. But as I rose this large group of mostly men in front of us stood. Are those your disciples from Oak Ridge?"

Bryon was amazed at this group that stood and identified themselves as my friend and family and it really touched his heart. He thought he would be the only one. They had been a powerful witness of Christian love and friendship. I could hardly wait until the next Sunday class to share this with the disciples. I wanted them to know how powerful their witness to Christ was in just the little things we do. As Christians we have nothing to prove as Christians, but by our quiet Christian deeds we show our Lord.

During the next week Paul and I shared the events of Mother's Day. He was so pleased for me and we talked about the next step. The next Sunday I would go forward at Crestview to join the church. I pulled my shy self out and asked him to walk with me. "It's something you need to do for yourself," he said. "It's okay; I will be there."

The invitation was extended by Dan and the music began to play. As the congregation sang I walked the aisle. Dan's eyes were kind and his reception warm. Many, many people came forward to greet me and so was to begin our fellowship as a Christian community.

God continued to unveil His plan for my life and I am so blessed that it includes my Crestview family and the disciples of Oak Ridge.

JOSHUA

This story has become a kind of tapestry of lives being woven together by God and it's becoming a bigger story of God's love and guidance. It may seem disjointed that I haven't shared the personal story of Joshua Harris, who is the founder of Oak Ridge Ministry. He has been clearly guided by God to plant this ministry and none of the rest of the story would exist without his story beginning. I have wrestled with conveying Joshua's personal story and tried several times filled with apprehension that I could do it justice. I have viewed the video over and over through tears and heard him give his testimony at the Ridge. It is so central to the vision of this ministry and the reason for its success that it is important to this story. I call it a "God wink" that Joshua was the one to whom God first led me. It is Joshua who lives his faith with such Christian integrity and touches so many lives with transformation. He is truly God's instrument. I felt inadequate to portray him as I really want you to know him. And so I prayed. God answered in another intriguing way.

One evening at Testify we were apprised of special guests. Michaela Cain, who writes for a local magazine, and her photographer Shelley Montgomery were to be our guests that night. Joshua informed the group of their presence and their purpose, saying that they would be gathering information for an article they would be writing for the Georgetown View Magazine. The article would appear on the stands in several months. Everyone was more than pleased that the wonderful story of Oak Ridge would be shared. And so it would be. I prefer to share Joshua story through Michaela's writing. This is taken from "Burying the Old Man," an article by Michaela Cain published in the Georgetown View Magazine in October 2014.

"In a field about forty-five minutes down a winding bumpy road west of Georgetown a man kneels to read a metal plaque. The tombstone bears the man's own name, cause of death, and when he died. Joshua Harris. Cocaine. May 22, 2005. When Joshua visits his tombstone today he remembers how it became the first of a long line of tombstones in this unusual graveyard, located in the middle of a former campground that is now part of a discipleship program for men with substance abuse: Oak Ridge Discipleship House. At Oak Ridge, Joshua helps men overcome addiction through his work. He's found that surrendering rather than changing behavioral habits often allows people to leave substance abuse behind.

Joshua's own story of his death starts with a vicious fight during what he had thought was a normal childhood. Ten-year-old Joshua hoisted himself up to look out his bedroom window. He'd heard a lot of yelling, and then the door slammed. He watched his father get in his car and drive down the road. Little did he know, as he watched the tail lights disappear, that he would never see his father again. All he knew was that his hero had left and that he was alone with his abusive stepmother.

This "step monster" beat Joshua daily with "high heels and brushes and anything that was close." His father, who had never touched him, was his source of comfort until the worst night of Joshua's life. "Did you ever have a time in your life that was so chaotic and crazy that you just felt like everything was moving in slow motion?" Joshua asked. "This night felt like that."

A few days after his father left Joshua learned that his father had been sexually abusing Joshua's 14-year-old sister for years, and she finally told her stepsisters, who told their mother about it. Soon after Joshua's dad left the stepmother, blaming the children in some way for the mess, kicked Joshua and his sister out. Joshua lived in an orphanage in Houston, estranged from his siblings, for the rest of his childhood. Years later, Joshua found out that his brother had also been a victim of their father's abuse.

When he was 19 years old, Joshua went out on his own "with a huge, gigantic hole in my heart and with a poor me chip on my shoulder as big as could be," Joshua said. "When you have a big sore on your heart, you'll do whatever you can to make it feel better." And for Joshua, that looked like using cocaine.

From the first time Joshua sniffed a line of white powder, when he was 21, he felt numb and lost. He began drinking as well and frequently would drive under the influence. One day, he got set up and busted for dealing drugs. When he got parole, Joshua returned to his old lifestyle. "For years I rode that roller coaster of drugs and alcohol and stealing and all of the things that come along with that life," he says. He tried to fake a drug test but didn't pass and was given five years of jail time, so he ran to Florida. While he was there, he says, "God put this conviction on me to come back." That feeling got stronger and stronger until he came back to Texas and turned himself in. "I said, 'I don't want to be a mess, I don't want to live like this anymore.' And I had said that lots of times throughout this process. But this was the first time I said, 'Lord Jesus, I don't want to live like this anymore,'" he recalls. He found a Gideon New

Testament and said, "If there is really a God who loves me, help me!"

He also met Pastor Bob Davis, who helped Joshua understand the Bible and invited Joshua to live with him when he got out. Joshua was stunned. He seized the opportunity and became a Christian to month after his release.

Everything looked better for many years. Joshua married and the couple had two children. But old wounds reopened. As a father himself, Joshua couldn't understand why his father had abused his older siblings and left him. He hired a company to find his dad. The search was successful, but two weeks before Joshua could meet with him, his father vanished again. Two weeks after that, Joshua was snorting cocaine again. For a year and a half, he returned to drug addiction, devastated by anger and a lack of closure. His wife left a voicemail saying he was not welcome at home nor in his children's lives. Intensely ashamed, he took enough cocaine, Dr. Slater told them, to have killed five men.

But instead of dying, he heard a voice asking him over and over, "Are you ready?" "Ready for what?" Joshua shouted. He felt the response: "Are you ready to change?" Then, Joshua says, "I heard God say audibly, 'Pick up the phone and call Pop,' which is what I called Bob Davis." He called and Bob answered saying, "Son, I been waiting for you to call for three weeks." He suggested that Joshua go to Denver City, Texas, to a six month discipleship facility called Trinity Baptist Men's Home. "When a man has come to the end of himself, when he's hit rock bottom and his spirit is broken — whether through drugs, alcohol, or other life hurts, habits, and hang-ups — he must be completely ready and willing to dedicate at least six months of his immediate future to burying his old former self and becoming a new creation through Christ Jesus," Joshua says.

That's exactly what happened at the discipleship home. Joshua attended chapel several times a day and memorized 45 Bible verses. One of the passages stood out to him: John 15:5, in which Jesus says, "I am the vine; you are the branches. If a man remains in Me and I in him, he will bear much fruit; apart from Me, you can do nothing." He believed that he needed to surrender to Christ in order to get free from addiction. At chapel one day, he literally said, "Jesus I'm not getting up from here until You take all this pain in my heart." For an hour, Joshua knelt in front of the chapel's altar, "crying, snorting and giving it up." He forgave those who had hurt him and let go of his anger toward his father — and when he got up, it was all gone — the pain, with the desire to ever use cocaine again.

The experience changed Joshua who wanted to offer a safe place for men to undergo the same transformation and freedom he felt at the altar. In 2009, he started

Oak Ridge Discipleship House, a residential Christian character — building course designed to remove old bad habits and develop good ones, to do just that. "We tried to remove, not so much by behavior modification, but by getting in their hearts and getting all the bad roots out," Joshua says the ultimate goal is for participants to heal relationships: with God, themselves, and others. They hope to conquer substance abuse and reunite their family — -just as Joshua was restored to his children and wife within a few months of leaving Trinity Baptist Discipleship Home.

Joshua was touched by another passage in Scripture in which Paul uses an analogy of burying an old lifestyle and starting a new one, and Joshua uses this passage to describe the type of surrender he experienced. The old man graveyard — what Joshua calls the "pride and joy" of the discipleship program — helps men encounter this mystical experience in a tangible way. It is important for the participants and their families to see their tombstone to provide closure on the old patterns and to give the man a chance to be a new person. Many of the men, including Joshua, take time every year to go back to look at their old tombstone and remember what God has done in their lives.

Currently, there are 57 engraved tombstones among the oak trees. Of the 57 graduates of the discipleship program, 75% continue to live substance free lives and

50% are involved in ministry. Joshua's goal is to see the "old man cemetery" filled — not to have accomplished the goal, but because the accomplishment would represent more people given new chances at life.

MEET YOU AT THE MORTUARY

"What are you talking about, Joshua? What do you mean?" I asked. Joshua had extended this invitation to Paul and me for Sunday morning. He grinned broadly and then took a moment to explain the seemingly strange meeting place for an Oak Ridge graduation. Then, it started to make sense. Ramsey Funeral Home offered the use of their chapel to Oak Ridge for holding graduation ceremonies for graduates of the program. Having learned the process of completing the program in which the men write a letter to their old man and figuratively bury their past and release it. They even are given engraved stones to place in the Oak Ridge cemetery as a reminder that their old life is gone and a new life has begun. As Joshua says, "You become a new man in Christ when you surrender to His will for your life. "

"I will give you a new heart and put a new spirit in you; I will remove from you your heart of stone and give you a heart of flesh." Ezekiel 36:26

We arrived at the mortuary shortly after our church service on Sunday. Other people were arriving and were also greeted at the door by a hostess, who directed us to the chapel. Friends and families of the graduates took their seats in pews near the front of the chapel. Supporters of the Ridge and other guests filed into the pews behind. The disciples, both current and former, were sitting in rows of chairs that were on the right side of the room, facing the center. The men who were to graduate were sitting in large arm chairs off to the left. Newly hewn grave stones, engraved with the graduates' names, sat atop wrought iron pedestals in the center of the room. It was solemn but impressive.

Joshua took his place behind the podium and greeted everyone. He opened with prayer, and we rose and sang hymns chosen by each graduate as his favorite. It's amazing how each song gives you more insight into that individual. After attending numerous graduations, I realized that I rarely heard the same scripture or song for another individual. They each chose a "life verse" that will be a constant resource of hope.

Joshua returned to the podium and gave a word of encouragement from the Bible. Then, Joshua looked squarely at the men who would soon graduate and face the biggest challenge of their lives and asked "Are you ready? Truly ready?" He gave them one more opportunity to indicate that it wasn't the right time yet. Joshua's pleading eyes inquired if each man was absolutely sure. In my heart, I know without a doubt there had been lots of preparation for this day, but that didn't minimize the magnitude of the challenge. Each of them affirmed their readiness and Joshua then turned to address the guests. "We give a charge to each man graduating. Each disciple in training along with graduates, staff members, and board members participate to give a word of encouragement biblically. To give a charge means to put a burden on."

"God is our refuge and strength, an ever-present help in trouble." Psalm 46:1

One by one disciples and staff and others in the Oak Ridge family stepped forward to deliver charges to the graduates. Each one was a very personal message which caused smiles as well as tears. Each spoke of the long fight for recovery that they had shared together as they learned to walk with Jesus. There were well wishes as well as warnings. I will never cease to be amazed by the words of wisdom that pour from these formerly addicted men who now walk in the kingdom of light. It would be impossible to share all the heartfelt messages conveyed over a number of graduation ceremonies represented here. However, Chester delivered a summary of charges that he put together at one ceremony. "I present to you the Oak Ridge formula for success: make good choices, listen, make time for God, pray, have faith, read God's Word, testify, encourage, be grateful, make every effort to be holy, worship the Creator, be prepared for spiritual battles, make no excuses, be faithful in small things, stay connected, be truly humble, be a leader, do not be afraid, serve, live with purpose, and focus on God. That's what matters most. We all have scars, but they're just reminders that we've been healed through Jesus Christ. Above all live your lives by loving God above all others and love your neighbor as yourself."

After all charges had been delivered, the next phase of graduation took center stage. Families of the graduates were invited to join them by the grave stones and in turn, Joshua enlisted support from them for holding the graduate accountable. The graduate then makes a pledge of accountability. The ceremony is closed with prayer.

There's always a specially made cake and punch to share after the ceremony. That gives ample time for guests to mingle and converse more intimately. And, mingle we do! There's a very real sense of family permeating the room. Yes, we are family of Oak Ridge, but also, members of the family of God.

I can't even begin to share the emotions that fill those moments. It's as if an ugly worm has been changed into a beautiful butterfly whose new life is just beginning. Yes, there are some tears, but they're overshadowed by broad smiles. Each graduation day is unique depending on the individuals—and doesn't that describe each of us? We're unique creations of God, created out of love. His love is unchangeable and He never gives up on anyone. You just have to ask Jesus into your heart and allow Him to be the light on your path. It's a very happy day.

NOT MY WAY, BUT HIS

It's been several years now since that change in my life and I've never looked back. I certainly never saw this coming, but God did. It was part of His plan in bringing me and others even closer to the ministry of Oak Ridge. In fact, when I look back on my entire life I can see how God has been the only constant in my life. He's unchangeable and ever loving. Life has been full of hills and valleys, twist and turns, dead ends and freeways. Satan and the evils of this world never give up challenging me, and I've made mistakes. I never could have predicted that I would be where I am at this point in my life. I've often fretted over not knowing what's next. But, I'm so relieved to tell you that it doesn't matter. I know how the story ends if I keep my eyes on Jesus. God sees sin as just sin. The boys are no better or worse than I as we all have a sinful nature. Now, they too have come from being totally broken to walking with Jesus. My prayer will always be that they keep their eyes on Jesus and lean their hearts to Him.

I always am anxious to see the boys on Wednesday and Sunday night. Joshua says he loves to be fed from the Word through Pastor Dan and Jack, our assistant minister. I know exactly what he means. If God's Word was arrows in Dan's quiver, then he would shoot them right straight through my heart on a regular basis. I am learning so much more than I ever thought possible. All three of our ministers deliver such spirit filled messages; and, I'm always amazed that the message is so timely. How can one message so appropriately address the need of each individual. I am struck by God's power to communicate through men devoted to God's service. I find my heart growing closer to God. I thirst for the feeding of God's word and the community of prayer and sharing. Joshua always says that victory comes through complete surrender to God. And I finally get it. Through all of this I too have been blessed by a fresh urgency to share my faith walk and God's love and desire for all to come to the knowledge of the truth. I have found community with God and a family of believers.

Never in my life did I think going to church would be something I really looked forward to doing. I was raised with the expectation that going to church and Sunday school was just something that was expected of you. Don't get me wrong; I most often enjoyed it once I was there and can say I personally benefitted from the teaching. However, there just wasn't that excitement. Now, I must admit that I am really anxious to go to church whenever the doors open attending Sunday services morning and evening as well as Wednesday prayer meeting and occasional Bible studies. Time and place makes a difference thankfully and I am impassioned with worship and learning.

Of course, my new church family helps make the difference for me. That would include the Oak Ridge Disciples who attend our services on Wednesday and Sunday evenings. The twelve faces have changed over the years but they're still "my boys."

Joshua often states that it's so good to be fed the Word of God in such a meaningful way by any of our three ministers. Dan is a master of Bible history with an art for relating lessons to today's world. Jack, is very picturesque and often uses humor to relate sound teaching. And then, there's Jordan, young and fresh who has a gift of relating to broad audiences. He's especially good at stepping on toes, but somehow you don't mind the correction. They all have so much to teach and really seek God's help in presenting relevant messages. Ok, I'm not as skilled as Jack, or Dan, or Jordan at relating God's message, but the words are in my heart.

One Wednesday Jack, our assistant minister, spoke directly to the Oak Ridge Disciples. Of course, it was a message for all of us but I could tell he had "the boys" on his heart. That day happened to be the anniversary of his own father's passing. What a heartfelt story he shared! With tears in his eyes he read a letter he wrote his own children the night before his own father died. There were other tears in the room as he described the character of this man to his own children. There was a core to the message that related so well to "the boys." Never throw up your hands and up. He referred to it as "calf rope," a phrase relating to cowboys at the rodeo during calf roping. You know they rope the calf and tie their legs and then throw up their hands to show they are through. It's a picturesque way of saying "Don't quit." Don't put in all the effort at a task and quit. Cross the finish line strong as Paul refers to in his epistle. Never give in and surrender when pursuing Christ. Your life depends on it. Your family depends on you. It's worth the effort. And God wants us to ditch our pride and become humble servants. "Do nothing out of selfish ambition or vain conceit, but in humility consider others better than yourselves." Philippians 2:3. Be humble because when you are the center of your universe there is no room for God. He's outside. There's no room for your loved ones and family who look to you. Be there as God's servant. "Man up" and become who God intended you to become and live in relationship with him.

This sermon in particular struck a chord with so many of the disciples especially. Oh, it hits us all for that matter. But I was especially moved by the reaction of the disciples who were able to hear it firsthand that night. As they complete their time at Oak Ridge and step out into a restored life there is celebration. After all, God brought them from a pit of despair and hopelessness into a restored life. Despite the euphoria of the moment of completion there is ample reason for caution. Joshua and others always reminds the guys that the challenge is just beginning and they will be given opportunity over and again to choose Jesus and stand strong. Satan will seek to destroy the new creation. And so, the stand needs to be taken. Don't quit! Don't throw all your efforts to the wind. Walk in God's way and don't give up! Make God the center of your universe! Man up!

I thank God for the many who have taken the challenge and fight the good fight! They do not waiver even though temptation comes. It's been with us since the garden of Eden.

The great majority of guys "man up" and meet the challenge. I thank God for each of them and their example. Some are far away in other states and we occasionally hear reports of them on Facebook or from others. Some even come back to visit. Some live near and we get the opportunity to see them. It is such a blessing to see how they are living and witnessing to the power of God. They have jobs, attend schools, create families and live as God intends.

I bet not one of them would tell you that he hasn't been challenged or tempted. They met the challenge! They have learned the right way but they each applied learning in their own style. In the next, chapter you'll meet a fine example of a young man who slowly but surely adapted to his new life and never lost sight of God.

SLOW BUT STEADY WINS

It was Friday morning and I was anxiously awaiting the arrival of Michelle. She is the mother of a former disciple who we know and love. We watched him progress on his walk through to becoming a new man at Oak Ridge Disciple House. But we actually knew very little about Erick. Though Erick has graduated, Michelle still continues to go to Testify and other Oak Ridge events and is a member of our circle of friends. She's an attractive, black-haired lady with a Christian heart. Her husband was killed in a motor accident; she makes her living as a housekeeper for people. Because of her work ethics and personality, she is in high demand. I was anxious for her to come over that Friday, not for one reason, but for two reasons.

First of all, I need to explain. Three months ago, Michelle showed up on my front doorstep with a mop in one hand and a bucket filled with cleaners in the other. "I've come to clean your house. It's my gift to you," she said. "You do so much for Oak Ridge." I was blown away at her generosity and offered to pay her, but she would not hear of it. She busied herself about her cleaning effort and we chatted as she worked away. Being better at giving than receiving, I was having difficulty with her generous offer. What a boost to my spirits that cleaning was! And an acquaintance became a friend.

This is the third time she has come to clean my house and I have come to reciprocate by doing some things for her. I was first looking forward to a sparkle and shine on my little house. It makes you feel so good when everything is clean, and cleaning has become more a burden as I age. Secondly, I had told her that I wanted to hear Erick's story. For some reason, Paul and I did not get to hear his testimony. New and exciting things were happening now in Erick's life and I wanted to know all about them.

That evening, Paul and I took Michelle out to dinner at an Italian restaurant in Georgetown. Though the menu was broad and filled with delicious offerings, we all settled on cannelloni. It was delicious and we talked as we ate. I was cautious to ask her if she'd rather tell her story when we went back to the house. "Oh no," Michelle's smiled. "I don't care if everybody hears. God has blessed us richly and it's a beautiful story." And so she began the tale of Erick.

"There are some awful hard words for a mother to hear," she began. Erick had told her he didn't believe in God. "I knew in my heart that it wasn't true, because of his writings. I had read the ones he wrote from a jail cell. He had called out to God. He knew without God there was no hope. Erick was only 21 when he finally entered Oak Ridge. It was a struggle to get to that point, but I knew that God held the only answer for turning Erick's life around."

As a mom she searched for the answer, for she knew a faith-based program was all that would work for Erick. All that she heard about were out-of-state and cost lots of money. She prayed and prayed. There is a real beauty in a mother's heart and her prayers.

She went to work at a Sun City home as was as her usual schedule. But little did she know what was in store for her. As she was cleaning the kitchen, the man of the house came in and just started talking to her for some reason. It felt very comfortable to talk with him. He asked about her children, and she told him she had a troubled son. Then out of the blue, the man started telling her about his volunteer work. It seems he does a lot of work with Oak Ridge Disciple House near Georgetown. He was out there very often and shared what a beneficial and God centered program it was. "It was as if God touched my heart and I blurted out, 'He's a heroin addict.' I could hardly wait to get home and call Joshua and I did. My head swirled with questions, 'Why did he ask me? Why did he ask about the youngest son? Is it really supposed to happen this way? Is God's hand really in this?" The answer to all my questions was yes.'"

"Erick wanted to be babied and coddled, but he got none of that from Joshua. In fact, Joshua was pretty intimidating, and rightfully so. God speaks truth and Joshua is a man of God. Erick shied off. No, he just flat refused to go using detox as his excuse. He said he would be very sick during withdrawal and that they wouldn't be able to help him. There was excuse after excuse for why he couldn't go to Oak Ridge." Michelle had been spending money — lots of money — and going without things as she tried to provide for Erick. She talked about taking him to a doctor to get him a special drug that would help him get off heroin, but little did she know what Erick was doing. Erick was actually selling the drug to buy heroin. She was going broke and Erick was getting deeper into his addiction. It was a vicious cycle that involved everyone in the family. His lifestyle led him to Miami, where he and some friends were not only making, but selling drugs. They were busted in Miami and Erick suddenly decided to come home in order to avoid arrest. Of course he didn't tell his mom why he had become so anxious to come home. The others in the group were arrested and are currently doing 30 years of hard time. Later, during his stay at Oak Ridge, Joshua would insist on him facing the charges against him and setting it right. He couldn't fly for fear of being arrested, so Joshua drove him to Florida to face the charges still pending against him and to answer for the crimes. No one ever knows how facing charges will ever come out because you're at the mercy of the court, but Joshua never lets it slide. It's part of the process. As Erick faced the judge, I am sure he was filled with fear, but he had lots of people praying for him. The gavel banged on the desk and the judge announced, "Free to go, time served. This is what we want to see. We want to see guys making things right, getting right with the law and staying clean. Going to jail is our only recourse for people who choose not to change."

There was a time when Erick was on the streets in Austin running drugs. While in a grocery store one night, he stole a candy bar. That seems insignificant enough, but he was caught and arrested. They searched his truck and found drugs. He was given the choice of going to jail or doing three months in a rehabilitation center in San Antonio. Of course, he chose rehab center to avoid jail. It was a regular rehab and it was their custom to take the guys to town and turn them loose during the day to find work. That doesn't sound like a very wise thing to me, nor did it to Michelle. But it was what it was! During one of those treks to town Erick secured some snack foods and brought them back onto the campus. That was against the rules. And so, Michelle was called in the middle of the night to come get him as he was kicked out of that rehab. Again Michelle pleaded for him to go to Oak Ridge. "I felt as if I was preaching to my son," Michelle said, "And I didn't really want to shove God in his throat since that wouldn't work." Erick continued to be persistent in saying, "There's no way I'm going." Michelle said she yelled and cried to God: "Why isn't this happening when I know it's what You want, God?" She said as she looked back, "It seemed like a black-and-white movie. All bleak. All good and evil in an opposing battle. Without God there is no color."

Erick's next big mistake was stealing checks from Michelle's checkbook. He forged the check for large sums of money and soon she was severely overdrawn and faced foreclosure of her home. Erick's disease had endangered everyone around him. It threatened to their very livelihood. So Michelle told Erick that he had no options. He had to go to Oak Ridge! "There were some things about that period of time that I didn't know about until I heard Erick's story at Testify. My older son really threatened Erick with a gun telling him he had to make things right. He had to go to Oak Ridge. The other option would have been awful, but things often end up like that in homes of addicts. Erick made the right choice. Erick made the God choice. He had come to the end of his rope. He called Joshua and asked. Joshua said, 'Yes, come.'"

It had been a vicious circle of gangs and guns and drugs for a long time. Much of it Michelle was totally unaware of until she heard Erick's testimony. But it had taken a toll on her life as well and put her security at risk. Michelle took Erick to the church where the disciples were that Tuesday evening. Every Tuesday evening, they participate in Celebrate Recovery. But that was the beginning for Erick and his round table was held there that evening. Joshua came to Michelle before she left and prayed with her. "Don't enable him," he said. "Let God take charge." And off Erick went in the van with the Oak Ridge disciples to what may have been his last chance.

Talk about a roller coaster of emotions! The families of these men certainly feel a myriad of things at the time their loved one enters Oak Ridge Disciple House. I'm always curious to hear their response when asked about the experience. But Michelle's answer quite surprised me. "I was at peace," Michelle said. "I never doubted that Erick was in the right place or that with God all things are possible. I had prayed for so long, so long for my son and I knew God loved Erick more than me. So now it was in His hands."

Paul and I didn't get well acquainted with Erick or his mother during the time he spent at the Ridge. He was there when we'd visit but seemed shy and reserved. He would smile but never really engaged with visitors. His mom was faithful to come out on Thursday. We didn't really get to know her well during his stay either. She was always pleasant and gave the impression she was filled with peace, joy and hope. In fact, we weren't at Erick's testimony or his graduation.

We were pleased to hear that he moved into transition house after graduation. He stayed connected to the disciples and involved in their activities. He had an inkling of where he wanted his life to go and I guess the boys knew.

The next thing we learned was that TJ and Erick had gone to an open house at Southwestern Baptist Theological Seminary in the Fort Worth area. It wasn't but a few months later and we heard that Erick was moving north and going to attend the seminary. Wow, that was amazing to us and we celebrated his commitment. But again we didn't have all the facts.

Michelle filled Paul and me in on the details at our visit in the restaurant. Erick felt he really needed to pursue the ministry. Talks about this school kept popping up and TJ had asked him to go to the open house with him. Erick said that he felt in his heart that he was supposed to be there. So, quiet Erick became bold. He went right over to the President of Southwestern and asked for a moment of his time to tell his story. Now, what are the chances of that happening with a hall filled with prospective students? Apparently it was the best chance because God was working through this opportunity. The man agreed to see him the next day and said he would be in touch. Sometimes there isn't follow through with people but such is not the case when God is involved. The next day the President of Southwestern sought Erick out across a room. This part reminds me of David in the Bible stepping out in bold faith knowing God was with him. Erick stepped into the office of that powerful man and boldly told his story, the whole story. As Erick was telling him how he wanted to learn and do God's work, the man sat at his desk writing on the back of his business card. He presented the card to Erick saying, "Take this to the business office. They'll know what to do." Erick read on the back of the card: FULL SCHOLARSHIP AWARDED. I'm sure his heart almost stopped. Mine would have. I know for a fact that this was an act of God.

So, Erick became a student at Southwestern Baptist Seminary. No, it wasn't easy. There have been bumps in the road and hurdles to jump. There are still lots of unknowns to face. That's life, especially when walking by faith. Experience has built character, empathy, persistence, and a strong prayer life. He can go forward with surefootedness, knowing God is with him.

A semester later Erick began to struggle with his decisions. University expectations were tough to reach and just living there had its own challenges and temptations. Keep in mind these guys are so new to this walk with God and sometimes falter. The big question is whether they can continue to lean on God for direction. Satan plays mind games. Pride gets in the picture, too. Sometimes knowing what to do is not as easy when you fear rejection and disappointment by fellow man. I've struggled all my life with hanging my own self-worth on what others think and it's not an easy habit to break. Erick left school and came home, but continued to struggle. God never gave up on Erick; He continues to love Erick in spite of his shortcomings. Fortunately, a good understanding of God and His grace offered to us through Jesus Christ still was anchored in Erick's heart. He's working with Christian friends, including Brandon, whose story will be shared in an upcoming chapter. Brandon has begun a Bible study and Erick is included in the group. I wouldn't be surprised at all to see a men's ministry develop out of this. In fact, it's on my heart and in my prayers and there are subtle revelations that lead me to think this. If you remember, I was the one who fulfilled God's purpose to teach when human doors were closed.

And Michelle? She's fine! No, she is more than fine! She is giving God glory for the things He has done in her family's life. She wants everyone to know how good God is and how He has all power to change what seems to be impossible to the possible. This mother never gave up on her child, but she was wise enough to know that you have to release your children to God. It's the hardest thing for a mother to see her son drowning in sin and know she was unable to save him from his choices. Thankfully, she knew God. Prayer does change things.

SIDE TRIP

The sun was beginning to set behind the trees as we arrived at the Ridge one Thursday evening. People meandered about the yard and happy chatter of visiting filled the air. Other supporters were also arriving and carried baskets or containers of food toward the house. Some disciples came toward us to help while others stirred about the porch visiting with guests. Climbing the steps and crossing the porch we entered the big living room also filled with people. Everyone seemed busy with visiting or preparing the meal. Then, my eyes fell on one single individual bent over working on something while he sat on the large couch. There were threads of many colors laying out on the coffee table before him and his hands quickly worked as his eyes were totally focused on what he was making. He seemed totally unaware of others in the room, preferring his isolation for the moment. He seemed to be of Hispanic descent with prominent

Side Trip

tattoos and a very short haircut. Finally, he looked up from his work and my eyes met his deep dark eyes, but there was not much expression on his face. Somehow he seemed sad and maybe a bit lonely. At least he gave that impression. Perhaps he just didn't know how to mingle with the group. We later came to know him as Joel, a recent arrival at Oak Ridge. We were not introduced to him as Joel, but for the life of me I cannot remember the name by which we first knew him. He changed his name to Joel much later in his stay at Oak Ridge when he assumed his identity as a new man in Christ. His craft was making woven crosses out of the many threads and putting them on a woven necklace. Joel was making necklaces almost every time we saw him. As he warmed up to the supporters, he began to talk with them a bit. He gave each of them a cross necklace he had made. It was to remind them how Jesus died on the cross to save them from certain eternal death; it was also his way of expressing gratitude for the kindness he was shown. As I remember Paul got a blue necklace and I was given a white one. It reminds me of Joel and Jesus every time I see it hanging by my vanity and I often wear it on special occasions. It's got to be very interesting to see the many crosses worn around people's necks that you met at church or at the Ridge. He was learning to testify by giving a gift with the saving message.

Joel warmed up and became friendlier as time passed; then, one day there was no tall, lanky Joel to be seen at the Ridge. Apparently someone from his past had made contact and talked him into leaving to go back to his previous life. We were very saddened to hear this news and still continued to pray for him. Not many guys ever took off once they were in the program, but occasionally there was one that just didn't fit. That profile just didn't seem to fit Joel, but the world has a strong pull on all of us. Every day we must decide who to serve. Choose Jesus.

I don't remember exactly how much time elapsed. It seems like maybe it was a month or so. Then again one Thursday evening we arrived to attend Testify only to be greeted by Joel, our prodigal son. He seemed most happy to be back and was glad to share his story. Yes, he'd been back to the world that tempted him; there had been some involvement with rival gangs. That alone scared him enough to know he had to come back. He had to continue what he had started. He had to stay away from that life. He had to begin a new life in Christ with Christian friends. "I was scared, Mama Kay. I thought they were going to kill me." Joel said earnestly. So, he ran back to safety. He ran to welcoming arms of Christian friends. He ran so he could live; and yes, he ran to Jesus. He was discovering on a deeper level how important it is to have a relationship with God and Christians to escape the evils of the world.

Joel continued to make crosses as gifts for the time he was there. There was an obvious change in him, too. He was happier to be there and more social than he'd ever been. He really did seem to be fitting in for the most part, but there must have been issues we didn't see or circumstances we didn't know about. It really doesn't matter. Joel left again. One Wednesday evening before church he came to us and told us that he was leaving the next day and we were very sad. Well, at least we were sad until we found out that Joshua was moving him to a disciple house at Conroe. It was Innerfaith Disciple House and was very much like Oak Ridge Disciple House. In fact, Chris, the director was a graduate of Oak Ridge. They, too, teach the three critical components of Christian character building. They are: Surrender, Obedience, and Service. The most important concept is developing a relationship with God on a personal level and coming to terms with himself as he really is. Only then can a man build relationships with others to embrace family, friends, church, and community. We said our goodbyes and I told Joel we would see him again. I don't think he believed me at that time but it seemed to please him. I reassured him that we would continue to pray on his behalf and wished him God's blessings in his new home.

And so, Joel moved to Conroe with those men and finished his discipleship there. He must have done a good job because he was asked to join the staff after graduation. That role he filled for some time. Actually, if memory serves me, I think maybe he and Chris grew up together or had been friends in the past. So it was a good relationship to foster. I do continue to hear from him on Facebook even now. He's no longer at Innerfaith Disciple House but he seems to still live in the same general area. From his post I can tell that sometimes he seems stressed by life and other times he's really happy. Aren't we all that way? He's just one of a number of disciple graduates with whom we still have contact. It's just amazing to see how their lives change and how they grow. I'm glad to report that most of them are doing well. Oh now, they still have the struggles of life as do we all and our loving God is there with each of them.

There's more to the story of Joel, but I must detour now to what may seem to be unrelated to Joel's story. I assure you it will end in a connection. I'm also sure you will see the hand of God written all over this.

One day Paul and I were walking in the neighborhoods close to our house just for pleasant exercise. Paul said, "I want to show you something I'm thinking about." It was then that we passed a house not too far from our neighborhood that had a for sale sign in the yard. I knew the house had been on the market for some time because I frequently drove down that road. However, it was nice to see that the owner had only recently chosen to renovate the property and bring any maintenance issues up-to-date. It was now a sparkling clean, very habitable little home just waiting for a new owner. As we walked around the property and peeked in the windows Paul offered his idea. "I think I want to make an offer on this house and see if I can buy it." Of course, my mind went to why he would do that when he already had such a darling little house very much like mine. He said, "I'd buy it as an investment and keep it as a rental property. You know banks aren't giving much interest on savings anymore and I need to grow this money I set aside for retirement."

Well, we talked about it on several occasions after that and I tried to dissuade him from buying a rent house. "Have you ever managed rental property, Paul?" was my question. In my married life in the valley, David and I had a number of rental properties. We had experience owning and managing rental property as a source of income. It was no bed of roses. In fact, it was hard work. Yes, we earned money, but we really worked for it and I wanted him to understand all the implications of that venture. Sometimes a property would barely pay for itself even though we were skilled at doing most of the work ourselves.

Then came another God wink. While checking my feed on Facebook one day I happened to notice an interesting post by another supporter of Oak Ridge. Because we had that connection I felt more interested in his post. It seemed his father had recently passed away and the family was trying to sell his property, a house. It was interesting enough that I decided to call him with Paul's idea for buying property in mind. At first, it didn't seem like a likely match because it was in Conroe. By the time I presented it to Paul for consideration, I was enthused. The house was the right price in a good neighborhood. It just happened to be a three-hour drive from us. Then, the seller offered a solution that seemed to make sense. He had a potential buyer that wanted the house. He was employed in a secure job and seemed responsible. Troubles had beset him which made getting an ordinary mortgage unlikely, but he still seemed qualified.

I gave Paul the information and contact information, adding, "You could buy the house and finance it for this prospective buyer if it all checks out. You'd have a great return on your investment, property to secure it, and no maintenance issues that would come with rental property."

Paul thought about it. As days passed Paul told me he had contacted the seller and was giving serious thought to it. He wanted us to go to Conroe and see the property and meet the prospective buyer. So, we

Side Trip

did just that. We were on the way to Conroe when we decided to make contact with Innerfaith to see if we could surprise Joel.

Chris at Innerfaith thought it was a great idea and told us when to come. We concluded our business with the realtor and met the buyer who wrote a contract with Paul. Paul also made and offer to buy the house. The end of that story is that everybody is happy. On a return trip, the whole business was complete. The heirs were happy. Paul had an investment with good returns. The young man had a new home.

Now back to our visit to Innerfaith in Conroe. We arrived and were met at the door by a very surprised Joel. Through his smiles he uttered, "They said I was having surprise visitors and I couldn't guess who would come see me. It's you! You said you would come and you did." Joel took us on a facility tour and introduced us to the disciples and staff. He seemed proud. "You have to tell them about the Bible Lady, Mama Kay," Joel pleaded. Nothing else would do to satisfy the curious onlookers so I gladly shared the story with these guys throwing in encouragement to be aware of God's subtle messages and guidance. Chris joined us and we enjoyed a visit with him. He took us on a tour of their cemetery for burying their old men which was filled with plaques for each individual who had committed his ways to Christ. It was inspiring and invigorating. "There's more to help," he said. Chris put a description of their work concisely. "Strengthening and establishing the inner man through faith in Christ Jesus, being rooted and established in the power of His love." Ephesians 3:14-21 What a true statement that was and how evident it was that God is working through this program, too. Shortly after that we left for the drive home. It had been a wonderful day. What a blessing it was to visit Innerfaith Disciple House in Conroe, TX.

HEART FOR MISSIONS

Paul and I met Brandon at Oak Ridge when he was still in discipleship. He was one of the youngest disciples we'd ever met. He's tall and slim with dark hair and deep, intriguing eyes. There was no smile on his face when we first met him; however, over time a smile has spread across his face from ear to ear. He was always soft-spoken, but seemed to be in deep thought. His parents and his brother came faithfully to Testify on Thursday nights while Brandon was in residence there. They were so filled with hope that this young man would be able to turn from his evil life into a life as a child of God. It gave Paul and me such pleasure to watch this youngster develop into a man, but more than that, it blessed us to see the Christian man he became. Brandon has a gift for writing and his words express so much sentiment reflecting to his journey that I'd like to share some of them.

"Do not assume you are God's child. We were all created by God, however, we are not all automatically God's children, and we are not all automatically saved. If you do not believe you can be a child of Satan, please read 1 John, chapter 3.

I walked around for twenty-one years being the child of Satan, the liar. Belief in Jesus makes you a child of God. When you become his child, you receive his spirit. This perfect spirit will reveal the lies in our life leading us to repentance due to our imperfect standards not matching with the perfect son of God (John 1:12). If you are a child of God, thank the Holy Spirit for testifying that you are God's child (Rom. 8:16). If you are not a child I pray you make the decision today to believe in Jesus Christ. Who is your father? Anyone who calls upon the name of the Lord, will be saved. If you have any questions, please message me and we can pray."

It's so difficult to find the words to share the depths of your heart and the sincere love of God you experience. Brandon does a beautiful job of this. And he's even written a poem:

"You are more than the choices you made.
You are more than your past mistakes.
In the name of Jesus, you've been saved.
You are new and you'll never see life the same.

The Lord will renew your heart to hate the things
He hates.
Romans chapter eight verse thirty-eight,
Nothing can come between you and the Father to
separate.
Even though that apple was not supposed to be eaten,
Adam and Eve sinned selfishly, and ate.
You must admit and accept you relate. Then,
quickly repent!
You'll begin to experience God's kingdom you're destined for, your fate!
There is evidence: this isn't fake.
Christ really did make the lame walk again.
Now it's your turn, 'Pick up your mat and walk.'
He said.
That same man, who demands, died and conquered
the grave.
Giving you grace, and sending the advocate.
Walk with Him, because He loves you and He's great.
Be grateful you're new and don't continue the same
mistakes.
Think about where you're going, not from where
you came.
Jesus is more powerful than your past.
'At the cross where I first saw the light,
And the burden of my heart rolled away,
It was there by faith,

I received my sight,
Now I am happy all the day.'
I tell you these things so you may experience
the same.
Thank the Lord for your circumstance,
Thank the Lord for your second chance.
Thank the Lord for a new life, given to us through
Jesus Christ.
Thank the Lord for making us new as these hard
hearts He chisels.
Thank the Lord for His unfailing love,
Shared with us directly from our mighty God above.
Thank the Lord for His peace,
And His overbearing power that brings us to
our knees.
Thank the Lord for His righteousness,
And the opportunity given to be next to Him.
Thank the Lord for sending His Son to Earth, He who
is greater than any pain and hurt."

That story that Brandon wrote about is the part we witness as disciples work their way through their stay at the Ridge. Only recently Brandon posted a video of his testimony online as a beacon of hope for the future to those who are struggling. What was Brandon's life before the Ridge? It's not pretty, but it's quite a tale. Brandon shared that he was a great kid with what seemed to him to be a normal childhood. He had been a good student in school and life was good. At some point he began to see how drug addiction destroyed his dad so he developed an attitude of hating the drug culture.

The influence from his peers was great and he decided just to try once so he could see "what the big deal was about." In his own words, he claims drugs had an immediate pull on him. After smoking weed, he began to mix pain killers and alcohol. He even drank cough syrup. By eighteen or nineteen he was consuming eighteen cans of beer a day. At that point he recalls that he had no hope, no joy, and he didn't care because he hated life so much. His days were busy in a life of crime to support his addiction. And, at night he would set out by his bed his next shot, dose, or whatever.

Life was survival in a world colored by drugs and alcohol. He showed up drunk at court one day and was sent home. He was fired from his job. On the way home he wrecked his car. He knew the police were summoned so he took all the pills he had and raced for home.

Brandon says, "God intervened because if I didn't go to jail and get cleaned up, I would have done it all again." He had found his rock bottom. Having already taken fifteen Xanax, he also took a mixture of thirty other pills and twenty Ambien. He was choosing to die.

But he remembers a small voice inside him whispered to call his mom, so he did. That became his lifeline. He vaguely remembers the police coming, as well as his dad, before he blacked out for two days. When he came back to reality days later he was given two choices because his parents knew they couldn't help him at home. He was given the choice to go to one of two places: Teen Challenge or Oak Ridge Disciple House. He took the first step to call "that man" at Oak Ridge who was Joshua Harris. "Come out tomorrow," Joshua said.

So, Brandon went. He tells it like this: "I said my first prayer that day to Jesus Christ and I actually heard the Gospel. I responded. My life has never been the same." He prayed, "Take this heart and change me. I'll do whatever it takes. Take my life." The result is heartwarming but not unusual on the Ridge. Brandon says, "I now have joy in my heart and hope in my life and a family who will never reject me." It's quite a contrast to think he no longer wakes up to ugly things by his bed. It's been replaced with the Bible.

Well, you know how life at the Ridge went for Brandon. He has a new heart that especially wants to share this joy and salvation with others who are in a fix like he was at one time. His plea is poignant: "Run to Jesus no matter who you are or where you're from or what you've done. God asks us to give all things up for Him and His work. So, don't hold on! Jesus is all that matters."

Heart For Missions

Brandon graduated and moved away for a short time. It wasn't long until he returned back to Georgetown and moved into an apartment with three other graduates. He got reconnected with Oak Ridge family and faithfully came to church at Crestview.

I'm not exactly sure how the connection happened but it's a good one. He soon was seen keeping company with Rachel, a young lady from our church. She has an amazing Christian family who accepted Brandon and loved him, too. I became better acquainted with Rachel and her mom so it expanded my family of Christian friends. Rachel and I both worked at Camp Crestview. One day at camp I ran into her when I was feeling stressed and she offered to pray with me. That made my day. What a beautiful soul!

At an Oak Ridge summer party, she shared with me how excited she was to be returning to Myanmar on a mission trip with our church. Brandon was to go on this mission trip, too. Pictures from their adventure in Myanmar were posted on social media and we followed them with interest. It was so apparent that God was moving in the hearts of those who went to serve, as well as in the hearts of the residents of Myanmar.

The first evening they were in church after the mission trip Pastor Dan called them out of the congregation to come and share about their trip. Together, they shyly came forward. Brandon begin to speak about his heart for missions in Myanmar until he was overwhelmed with emotion to the point of tears. Rachel stepped in, and continued where he had left off, sharing stories of planting seeds of God's word in the hearts of Myanmar children and adults. Brandon used the time that Rachel was sharing to compose himself and was then able to share some touching stories of sharing Jesus and witnessing people's acceptance of the Gospel. He and Rachel truly have hearts for mission work.

Several weeks later, Brandon and the Myanmar mission team all came to the Ridge for Testify to share their story. They call it "Love for Myanmar" and they told wonderful stories of their work in the country that used to be called Burma. Brandon closed the evening of guest speakers with his own story. As a cool evening breeze blew, he made his invitation to work in the mission fields wherever God calls you. The darkness of night surrounded us as he spoke, but on that porch we had the only light visible. "This little light of mine, I'm going to let it shine." God calls us to shine and spread hope and love in the world.

WHERE HE CALLS, THEY GO

The story of Brandon brings to mind another disciple graduate with a common interest. Jared was a burly young man from Louisiana who found Jesus at Oak Ridge and fell in love with Him. When Jared began to smile it just wouldn't stop. He was so personable that it was difficult to imagine a dark past in this young life. Yet he, too, would be called to missions. In reality all of us are called to share the story of salvation with others. Their callings would involve world travel.

Jared and another disciple, Colbert always came to meet us when we went out there. It was probably to see if I'd brought any Cajun cooking for them. They loved it and I enjoy spoiling them a bit with familiar cooking. You see, Colbert is from the border between Texas and Louisiana in swamp country. Jared came to the Ridge from Baton Rouge, Louisiana. I, too, love Cajun cooking and music. My husband even had a Cajun accordion that was made for him in Lafayette. So the boys and I found a common ground of interest.

Jared's troubles were not unlike other disciples that came before, but I took particular interest in the way he came to Oak Ridge. He claims to be his father's son in a proud way. His daddy had seen him through the best and the worst and loved him in spite of everything. It was his dad who had diligently sought help for Jared, even reaching back in their past. Fortunately, he reached out to a lady in Georgetown, who had been one of Jared's favorite school teachers. I never cease to be amazed at God's connections. It was through this teacher that parents connected with this Christian character building program and Jared met God.

Ms. Jane, Jared's favorite teacher from years ago, is a member of First Baptist church, the home church of Oak Ridge Disciple House, as well as an avid supporter of Joshua's ministry. Perhaps you would agree with me that God's guidance was in it when Jared's dad reached out to Ms. Jane many miles from his home in Louisiana.

Jared had graduated with top honors from high school and thus was afforded a full college scholarship. It was evident that he was very bright and cute, but Jared had deep secrets of addiction. Being a member of an "animal house" fraternity with no roommate to keep tabs and no one to answer to fostered lots of foolishness. His 4.0 grade average gave him even more reason to be a self-assured, self-centered loner who had decided he could not fail. He was out of control and in time his lifestyle choices took a toll; he had to answer for his ways with the law. Depression became his next attacker.

Dad had enlisted the help of friends and prayer partners and when it was God's time, Jared was touched. Jared says the first sermon he heard was on discipleship. I had to grin at that comment. He said it was what he needed to hear. The seed was planted to be full in its season at Oak Ridge. Long-haired, bearded Jared agreed to come to Texas knowing only that it was near Austin and to him, Austin meant 6th Street, the center of the party life. The crowd begin to giggle knowingly as they shared in the joke. Yes, it was near Austin, but he came thirty miles north to Georgetown only to find he had to go even farther away from Austin. And then, he had his own personal experience on the "Damascus Road" on the way to Oak Ridge. I guess you recall my mention of the long drive to the Ridge. So began his discipleship and through God's saving grace he came to graduate here before returning to graduate from Tulane. Jared graduated, and pursued his plans. He would return to Louisiana where he would complete his last semester in the university to earn his degree in petroleum engineering.

The Thursday before graduation Jared stepped before the crowd on the deck of the Ridge to share his story. I shall never forget his choice of songs for the evening as it totally paints a picture of Jared and the Ridge, which Joshua often refers to as the mountain. We all sang:

Up on the mountain
Where your love captured me
Where finally I'm free
This I know . . .
Up on the mountain
Where You taught my soul to sing
Amazing grace, the sweetest thing,
This I know . . .
Take me up to where I was
When I never wanted more than you
Lift me up to feel your touch
It wouldn't be that much for You
This I know . . .
Up on the mountain
Where you took my hand
Taught me to dance again
This I know . . .
Up on the mountain
Where you took this heart of stone
Put life back in these bones
This I know

His eyes twinkled the next time we saw him on a visit. "I have my degree and plan to pursue my career abroad." Then, he added the amazing part. That travel abroad would also allow him opportunity to share Jesus and the path of salvation with the world and that was his heart. He, too, had been given a heart for missions.

VISITOR FROM THE PAST

Sunday night many family members and supporters gather with the group among other worshippers to join in worship. Often there are faces from the past that come back. We keep in touch with a number of graduates and are always glad to see them. Some we frankly lose track of as they test their new wings in a real world. It would be naive to think all succeed; however, there is an exceptionally high success rate in this ministry. They are human. Haven't we all met challenges to our faith and godly lives? There is always reason to celebrate when the ones you've lost touch with return to the fold. "Consider it pure joy, my brothers, whenever you face trials of many kinds, because you know that the testing of your faith develops perseverance." James 1:2-3

Well, one Sunday evening Paul and I entered the church anxious to get to our usual seats. To my left I caught sight of a broad smile and bald head. Whoa! I did a double take as I as realized it was RC and he was accompanied by his lovely wife. He had struggled after leaving Oakridge but the teaching had taken root. It was so good to see him and his new wife and catch up on events. But it was cause for great thanksgiving to hear that he was meeting with Joshua and was finding his way to reconstruct his life to be God's servant. That smile was always a winner but it was even brighter that night.

RC had been one of the first disciples we met at Oak Ridge. His story was not unlike many others with a life ruined by drugs and alcohol. His appearance was striking. He was tall and strong with a bold chain tattoo that encircled his neck. It was not unusual to see ink on the boys, but that was especially striking and bold. Paul and I wondered how it would affect him in the work world. I know we are old fashioned by today's standards but employers do consider it. We've come to love and accept RC just as he is as we got acquainted.

I will never forget sitting with him on the deck over the Ridge one cold winter night. Several of us huddled by a porch heater as he related a personal story. In his own words he admitted how he hadn't been able to read and it really hurt him that he couldn't even read a book to his children. This man's story has a blessed ending though. You see, the disciples had taught him to read and it gave him the greatest pleasure to read with his kids on a visit home. I'll never forget the tears in those wide eyes or the even brighter smile that night. It really hurt me since I'd spent most of my career teaching kids to read. A friend of mine, Barbara, who had accompanied us to the Ridge that night sat with us. She still recounts fondly his story whenever I bring up the disciples. It's just one example of how the story of the disciples touches the hearts of people. She still prays for these men and so the prayer circle continues to expand.

The rest of the story? Well, it's not good yet, but we have hope. I finally deleted RC from my social media because it wasn't good and godly; it was another turn for the worse and another trap by Satan, who never gives up. The world is a hard place to live a godly life. We're shaped by our past but it doesn't have to become our future if we allow God in our present.

His mother is still a social media friend and I periodically touch base with her. Recently, I began leading a group of women in a study of the book, *Becoming Myself: Embracing God's Dream of You*, by Stasi Eldredge. Ann, RC's mother, called me expressing an interest in the study. She hasn't been able to attend but planned to get the book and study herself. She also caught me up to date with RC and it's a rough story. RC lost his way again and fell into crime and the dark world that he'd known so well. It's so easy to fall because Satan really attacks these guys. Satan isn't pleased that they found a new life in Jesus. After all, most of their lives were spent surviving in that dark world and the Christian walk was new. Thank God the seed of the gospel is planted deep inside each graduate and can again spring to life in Christ. RC had a tough lesson in accountability and is spending several years in prison. Is there hope? Definitely, without seeing I make that statement, but I have been given knowledge. Ann tells me he is trying to get placed in the Christian quarters of the prison and is attending Bible classes and sharing his faith. Praise God for always being available and willing.

LET'S HAVE A BURGER

*D*own the steps of the church we headed for the car, looking forward to meeting our couple friends at a local hamburger place. It was Sunday evening and we had just been blessed by the message at the Alive Worship Service. And as we are creatures of habit we knew the plan to meet at the same place every week to eat and chat. It was my extreme pleasure to gather in community with these Christian friends. We often invited friends we met through Oak Ridge to join us. We love incorporating believers into our other circle of church friends. And, sometimes the guests would share their connection to Oak Ridge or their own testimony.

This group had been Paul's friends for many years but it hadn't taken long for me to assimilate into the group. I remember the first time he asked me to go there after church on Sunday evening and it brings a smile. Of course, I accepted the invite quickly. But then, Paul tucked his head a bit and looked somewhat sheepish as he made the next statement. "The men usually sit together at one table and talk football," he explained. "And the women usually sit together and talk about the men." I had to chuckle. He quickly added, "But I can sit with you if you'd rather." I quickly agreed that it would be fine for him to sit with his buds as was their custom but I have to admit that I was somewhat apprehensive about eating with a group of church women I barely knew.

My fears were soon banished as I was quickly welcomed into the group. As weeks turned into months I felt very much a part of this group of Christian ladies. Sometimes there were as few as four ladies but that was rare. Most nights there were eight to ten women and sometimes even more. And it was obvious from the laughter that rose from the men's table that they too were having fun. And, it's worth noting that the women do find more to discuss than talking about the men.

We often chatted about their families and travels as each one took a personal interest in each other. It seemed someone was always going or returning from adventures. Some were just trips to see family and attend events but it's remarkable how much fun we oldsters can incorporate into our lives. They kid Dianne about spending so much time traveling to Florida and Colorado and other places that she sleeps more away from her home than in it. Others took a 50th anniversary trips to Nova Scotia. There are two couples who share the wedding anniversary on the same day and have for fifty years. Sweet Marie often goes to visit family a day's drive away, but agonizes over how much it hurts Joe, who can't travel now. Several own recreational vehicles and go camping or travel to the beach. It's even rumored that one couple has pink inner tubes they use to float down Texas Rivers. That just has to be fun.

There is one sanctioned event that is never missed by the men in the group. It's Cowboy Night hosted by Pam and Bob. It happens the first Tuesday of every month at their home where Pam plays hostess and spoils the guys with tasty desserts. It's a group of seven men because that's how many viewing chairs there are for the two cowboy flicks that are shown. Bob has an unimaginable collection of old movies that they watch. Most nights the other women go separate ways and do what pleases them since their man is occupied. But on several occasions we have gathered to watch chick flicks and totally enjoyed the evening together.

Our gal group supports each other so well. One example of this is Lana's story. Lana works in the special needs classes at the high school, but she'll quickly tell you she does that to support her annual mission trips to India. She works with the women in several Indian villages to share the message of salvation and her love of Christ. She prepares gifts and crafts for the women and children all year in anticipation of her visit. Needless to say, her baggage expense alone is significant. The ladies in our group all help her gather and make things for her trips and we have so much fun. It's such a treat to see the pictures she returns with of the women and children with our crafts and gifts.

New people have joined the group of regulars over the last several years. Suffice to say that I would lose you in the maze if I tried to describe the connection we each have with another. Paul and I probably spend more time with recent newcomers, Sharon and Jerry because they too are focused on supporting the work of Oak Ridge Ministries. Their son, Ben, often bakes cakes for the disciples for the Thursday dinner at the Ridge. Jerry has become the designated driver to carry a van load of us to Thursday Testify and Sharon lovingly prepares casseroles to share. With every seat occupied, the back end loaded with home-cooked dishes, and Ben squeezed between the two people in the back, we set off on our drive Oak Ridge with anticipation of an evening with God's people. It's interesting to see newcomers develop close relationships with the disciples and this ministry in the same way we did. God is really bringing people together.

Well, this was to be an Oak Ridge story but I got sidetracked as old ladies often do. While it is important for you to know about my Christian walk and my life, it is most important to me to share the Oak Ridge story.

When I started the part of the story about "let's have a burger" evenings I was headed toward another goal but missed a turn. Let's go back to exiting church one Sunday evening. We descended the steps only to be surprised by big hugs and exuberant greetings from our friends John and Kym and their kids. John, one of the graduate disciples, and his wife Kym and their kiddos chattered away with us. Eli, their three-year-old, was in daddy's arms. Kym's teenage kids were with them, too. The whole family had come from San Antonio to worship with their disciple friends and visit. The disciples and their families and friends attend worship at Crestview on Sunday evenings while attending their home church, First Baptist, in the morning.

It was so good to see them here. They agreed to meet us for burgers so we could visit more. Our group that night grew significantly, but I was really happy to be able to share some of the Oak Ridge story with our group of customary diners. Eli was attracted to the ladybug screen saver on my phone. It would flip its wings when you touched the screen. He busied himself showing his ladybug to other guests which left us free to chat.

John had recently given his testimony at the ridge and graduated to return to his family. His testimony had threads of similarities to those we'd heard before. John was raised in a Christian home but had lost his way and been consumed with addiction to the point of even breaking in places to secure funds to feed his habit. After much prayer, Kym had finally driven John to the Ridge in final hope for help. We had to chuckle at the picture created in our minds of his arrival at the Ridge. Kym had driven him there stuffed in the back of a very tiny car. The thought of this "John sausage" bumping down the Ridge road to an unknown destination with confusion and fear in his mind made for an amusing moment. It takes Jesus to overcome and Joshua says the men have to be totally broken for God to do His best work. So He would. This time He would restore a family, or so it seemed.

It would be so nice to say that life was now perfect for John and his beautiful family. That was not the whole picture. John still owed a debt to society. On the church steps that night he told us how much he loved being with his family again and healed through Christ. But, he had reason for serious concern. Time would tell if he would be held accountable for ten years of prison time. He had lots of serious obligations to face. Only time and a lot of prayer would reveal God's plan for mercy but it was not without "God moments" for John.

We kept in touch with them through texting and news from the Ridge. There was no word and time passed as did court dates. Finally, he was incarcerated in a facility in another county. He was not there long before a message came from Kym: "John needs ten Bibles. They must be paperback." That was the message.

Of course, I was intrigued and asked "What's going on? Isn't he in jail?" The return story warmed my heart. What an opportunity he had been given by God and he did not hesitate to act for God. John had been talking about God and Jesus with his fellow inmates. He had even started a Bible study and the listeners were ready to participate. Wow! That just blew me away. God is amazing and He can work through any situation. He loves His creation and wants all men to be saved and come to knowledge of truth.

It didn't take long before the next part of the story would be revealed. The wait for a verdict was over and with amazement we heard the news. John was released! His debt would be paid through fines, public service, classes and someone to answer to for a period of time, but he could go home to the family he loved. And so he did!

Life is just a series of lessons on the way to a Savior who loves us. On another visit I would become painfully aware of the struggles of putting a family and marriage back together. But that would come from another source.

A WIFE'S HEART

Graduation was approaching again for another group of graduates and we were at Testify to hear another story of redemption and salvation. This night became special in another way as we arrived. We were delighted to see Kym and John arrive from San Antonio to participate in the evening activities. Excitement ensued as we welcomed them back to the family of Oak Ridge. As the conversation progressed it was evident they wanted to come back for graduation weekend but had no idea where they would stay if they came to graduation two weeks away. They wanted to come on Saturday so John could spend some time with the guys and go to several projects with them. I was totally delighted when they agreed to accept my invitation to stay with me that weekend.

The much anticipated weekend arrived and I was so excited to have overnight guests. I had a booth at a craft show on Saturday but was really ready for it to be over by four that afternoon. It had been fun meeting people and marketing my wares but I'm not as young and able as I used to be when I did this on a regular basis with my husband years ago. I quickly figured out that it wasn't a piece of cake like it had been in the past. Bryon, my son, and Paul showed up early to set up the canopy and unload all the merchandise. We had packed up the day before and arrived early with two vehicles, both filled with goodies that we had picked up from my little boutique, as well as set-up equipment from the garage. Bryon had been well-trained in how to set up for shows by his dad and had helped us many times. Paul was a willing worker and was lots of help. My job was to set up displays and do the selling.

    The day seemed longer than I remembered but that too probably has to do with age. As time came to close down and pack, I was definitely ready. Fortunately, Paul and Bryon returned to tear down and pack up; John and Kym also showed up at the fair grounds to help. We'd been texting during the day and I was so glad to see them. James, another disciple, and his wife Rachael also came. He would be graduating on Sunday and was spending time with his family who came for the celebration. Both disciples jumped in to help us. The men made quick work of the packing and we were on our way.

Kym and John, along with three-year-old Eli followed me to the house and the visiting began. I was most happy to crawl into my recliner with a big glass of tea and rest while talking to my dear friends. I was filled with anticipation that John would tell me more about his story to add to my developing story. But that isn't what God had in mind.

Kym was to become the next part of this story. She wasn't feeling well and needed to rest so she took up residency in my companion recliner and our chat began. John took up occupying the time of a busy, curious three-year-old and that required energy. They decided not to go to Austin Stone Church that evening and to just relax instead. John took Eli to the playground across the street while Kym and I chatted. I'm sure we ate as I never miss a meal, but, frankly, I don't remember much besides my intriguing talk with Kym.

In the wee hours of the morning, Kym and I reluctantly went to bed. Hours had passed and my mind was whirling as a result of our discussion. It was as if God had opened a curtain to expose an expanding view of the story of Oak Ridge. I had been so totally focused on the disciples and their regeneration in Christ that I was oblivious to more than a surface view of the plight of the families of these men.

Hallelujah! The men had hit rock bottom and brokenness enough to reach out to God and salvation through Jesus Christ. It was true. Lives were amazingly changed through the power of the Holy Spirit. The same physical embodiment of these men was not the same as the man who graduated. Paul and I had witnessed the transformation of individuals which was drastic and beautiful. It was awe inspiring.

Yet many of them longed now to return to families who loved them. Many, like John, had not so damaged his relationship with his family that it was not salvageable. Kym's faith and prayerful support kept her desire to rebuild a family strong. For hours she had poured out her heart telling me about the hurdles they had to cross. I was dumbfounded by her statement, "You know, Kay, he is not the same man who left home over six months ago to begin his work at Oak Ridge. His body came home but the contents of his heart have changed. He was a stranger in many ways." Any change is difficult. Even good changes require adjustment. Fortunately, Kym had grown with John and was facing the challenge with God as a partner.

Every couple is different and not every wife is ready to meet their partner on the new ground of faith. Having been close to alcoholism in members of my own family, I could relate personally. Individual attributes and circumstances lead each person in the relationship to react the way they choose. Of course, the relationship with

Christ is the key to success. But no one ever claimed it to be easy. God can and does work in all things.

Struggles were a fact of life. Their whole lives had been turned over and over with personal struggles, extended family interaction, legal implications, and income difficulties. Consideration for children added to the mix. Everyone had been torn apart and tossed about to the point of exhaustion.

The disciple had exited the safe, secure home he found at Oak Ridge. This was his heart's desire and dream to re-enter the real world with his family; he had longed for this day. His every waking hour at the Ridge had been totally focused on Jesus, the Savior, and the Christian walk. From rising very early for praise and worship and Bible study to closing the day in the same manner, they lived immersed in Christ. Walking a Christian walk of servanthood was a daily thing and hard work was expected. His total responsibility was walking with Christ and learning how to serve others.

Kym shared another thought that touched my heart. "We, the families, are so glad they are there and getting help. Some are willing to totally walk away and go on with life without them. Some of us choose to hang in there. But as thankful as we are, and as relieved as we are, there is the reality of our lives going on and it's a struggle. They don't have to be concerned with mounting bills, housing expenses, food on the table, nourishing kids, and fighting every battle that we face on a daily basis. It's hard. It can be almost impossible. We have mounting debts and expenses of living and children to parent. I gave up my job to raise my kids and meet the demands being placed on me. It was stress city."

It was a new revelation to me about the struggles these families face. Addiction and crime don't just affect individuals. They tear up families. It isn't just suddenly rosy with a picture perfect situation when the guys graduate. It's just the beginning of a new process to grow together as a couple as God designed marriage. There's more work to do repairing damaged relationships, becoming financially responsible, building trust and just living a new life. With this realization came another piece of the puzzle.

MINISTRY TO WOMEN

I had new eyes after that talk with Kym and I had a new prayer concern on my heart. I thought about the women and the families so much after that. It was like someone had turned on another light in the room of my mind, but I didn't know where it was taking me until sometime later. I just devoted extra prayer time to these individuals and families.

The answer was to come to my heart one night at Testify. Worship was in progress that night and we were singing. Suddenly but surely the words of God came upon my heart and into my mind. "Ministry for the women of Oak Ridge!" That was the command! "But how?" I thought. The thought persisted and grew over the coming weeks, but I still didn't know how it was to be accomplished. God has called me to act before and that first step is the scariest. It's called faith and willingness to let God lead.

One day, I called Kym to tell her what was going on. I was apprehensive, but she melted with appreciation and confirmation of the need. Over the phone we explored what that ministry might look like. It was something like finding out you're having a baby but don't know how it will grow and what your part is in that process.

I had to talk with Joshua, but had concerns about bringing up the topic. Oak Ridge was his calling and ministry and it was great. It was definitely a God-centered program. Joshua had very definite ideas of his mission and how it evolved. I was concerned to express my ideas as I didn't want to interfere with the plan, vision, and ministry that God was clearly already using.

One evening I asked Joshua if I could have a coffee for the wives and mothers of the disciples. I wanted to do something for them, too. He said sure, and didn't think twice. However, he let me know that other ladies were also befriending these women. I didn't chase that thought. I just kept moving forward.

On Thursday night he gave me the floor to address the gathering which included disciples, families, and supporters. "Okay, Heavenly Father, we're up to bat. I quickly gathered my thoughts and with a short explanation I extended an invitation to the women of Oak Ridge to join me for coffee and fellowship on Saturday morning at my house.

The reception of my ideas was gratifying and I had a number of confirmations that they would come. Both supporters and the women themselves seemed pleased to attend and welcomed the idea. Some gave excuses for this time but asked me to keep them informed.

God has a wonderful way of communicating confirmation that we're in His will. Later in the evening Debbie came to me and laid that confirmation on me. "Another lady and I were just talking about this need and have even addressed it with Joshua. I'll be there." Wow, that was three minds having the same thought. So, on we go.

Saturday morning came and so did the ladies. There were mothers and wives of disciples as well as supporters, prayer partners, and even a member of the board who would partner with me in this endeavor. There were about fifteen of us in that first fellowship. We sipped coffee and lemonade while munching on goodies. Almost everyone had arrived with sweet treats to share. That always makes the conversation more inviting.

Then, we gathered in a huge circle to pray and discuss this new venture. Everyone had an opportunity to share their ideas of this ministry group and what it could offer the women of Oak Ridge. It was exciting to see how the ladies felt and how they were willing to become involved. Plans and ideas were jotted in a notebook to be presented to Joshua for his approval. That meeting with Joshua, Debbie, Jodilynn, and I took place about a week later over dinner. Then, we moved forward within the guidelines he set.

    A number of get-togethers were held and each had its own unique character. For each event I tried to have a theme and purpose that would be meaningful. We had brunch one time and snacks another. We even went out to lunch together. I think they call it bonding. I presented an inspirational topic and then we just talked and talked. In addition, we opened lines of communication with each other that included supportive phone calls and prayers. I was blessed by the testimonies they shared and the love they expressed for each other. It was wonderful in a blessed way to see tears release pain as we turned to our Father in Heaven. Hope was a gift that was shared. It was just comforting not to be alone. We became known as the "Circle of Friends" inspired by a song by Point of Grace.

"We were made to love and be loved
But the price this world demands
Will cost you far too much
I spent so many years just trying to fit in
Now I've found a place in this circle of friends
In a circle of friends, we have one Father
In a circle of friends, we share this prayer

That every orphaned soul will know and all will enter in
To the shelter of this circle of friends
If you weep, I will weep with you
And if you sing for joy the rest of us will lift our voices too
And no matter what you feel inside
There's no need to pretend
That's the way it is in this circle of friends
In a circle of friends, we have one Father
In a circle of friends, we share this prayer
That we'll gather together no matter how the highway bends
I will not lose this circle of friends"

Never doubt that if three or more are gathered in God's name He will be in the midst of them. I really tried to follow God's leading, but I must admit I sometimes got frustrated when events didn't quite seem to go as I thought they should. I have a little experience about that to share with you. It was Valentine's Day and it fell on Saturday, our usual meeting day. Some people wanted me to reschedule due to the holiday. Being as strong minded as I am, I resisted saying, "It's a good day to celebrate God's love. Especially if you are alone or hurting." And so, I planned the event so that it would include receiving valentines from Jesus as well as writing our own love letters to Jesus, sharing the concerns of our hearts. Each lady thoughtfully wrote her letter on rose bordered paper and it was sealed and placed in an offering box. The topic of the day was to be "A Mother's Love." I planned to share a story I'd written of the mother of a disciple.

As ladies began to arrive, I was overcome with an uneasy feeling that there weren't as many of us as in previous groups. I allowed myself at that point to become disappointed. But, the show must go on, and so we proceeded. As I started to deliver the story of the disciple's mother it suddenly dawned on me as if God turned on a light bulb. The room was graced by mothers—just mothers! Yes, God had a plan.

DESIRE TO MARRY

Our disciples come from homes with different family members and living arrangements though all have been through the torment of addiction. As Kym had shared so openly with me, I became alarmingly aware of the needs of couples. While some disciples have totally alienated their families, others have high hopes of reestablishing a connection with the woman in their previous lives. Some of them have children and desire to become partners with the mother of their children. Debra, Jodilynn, and I were all impressed with the need to care for the families, wives and mothers of the disciples. God had touched each of our hearts with a bid to service. It also gave us a better chance to establish friendships. It was about the same time that there happened to be two young couples in the program. Unlike many couples, these families lived in this area which alleviated the stress many face over distance.

Even between these two couples there were stark differences but common desires.

Well, the guys were disciples during the same time period and the wives were often at Testify. Though they appeared to be very similar in many ways they were different with different needs to reestablish their families. Both graduated from the Ridge on the same Sunday and re-entered the world as couples. Each made the same promise to his wife and children and others to follow the plan for his newly established life in Jesus. Families promised to hold their disciples accountable. And after lots of praise and testimony—happy, happy, happy! Or not . . . It's a real world out there.

Joe's wife and children were at Testify and other gatherings and it was obvious how hopeful and joyful they were that Joe had made this change. I was told that Megan's heart had softened as the program progressed. Apparently, she was totally fed up and in process of filing for divorce when Joe was brought to the Ridge. Joe's wife had been total support for the family which included two children. Like other wives she had struggled financially and emotionally having been abandoned by her partner who was plagued with addiction. Megan is a beautiful, round faced woman who exudes joy. It's hard to imagine now that she was so broken. She's very creative, outgoing, and determined. This became quickly evident. I was so glad she came to the first Circle of Friends and participated in the lively conversation. Before the end of that day she had offered to help me with a project. I was trying to set up an online store and was frustrated. She is blessed with a servant heart and so showed up another Saturday to work with me and accomplish the task. The task was accomplished quickly over a few hours and I got to know her better. She has a serious online business presence and operates a boutique operation for children. It was amazing to hear of her import operation from other countries, inventory and warehousing merchandise, pretty things created to sell, and orders received through her online store. I was amazed as I sat there thinking of the hours she spent with her business providing for her family. And she still found time to devote to her two beautiful children. It was still tight at times and she was anticipating Joe rejoining the family soon.

Graduation came and Joe went home. I saw him one Friday at lunch with the graduates. They call it accountability lunch because they can come back to be with their brothers in Christ. He said he was still searching for a permanent job, but had been able to find some work in building, remodeling, and contracting services, which was an area in which he was skilled. He was not the only one to face the challenge of trying to establish trust at work, due to his checkered past. He said that he'd also been helping his wife in the warehouse and things he could do for her business. I know she loved that. Later, Joe would become very busy with remodeling and building. He still takes an active role in the Ridge showing up with doors to replace or a turkey for the holidays. He takes an active role in providing for his family and serving others. And, they would be welcoming a new baby into their family in the near future.

The other couple lived together and have a small child. She is the most beautiful little girl and obviously the apple of her daddy's eye. A week before graduation we celebrated their union in marriage at the Ridge. Trey had obviously known her for long enough to have a history and a child. He was anxious to make them a real family as soon as possible. She and the other ladies pulled together an amazing wedding in a very short amount of time. The wedding was held at the Ridge the day after Trey gave his testimony at the Ridge. Cars once again traveled the rocky road to the happy event. Excited friends and family arrived with gifts and food for the meal. Final touches were put on a wedding cake with real roses. The decks were full of tables set up for dining. On the grassy ridge overlooking an expanse of tree covered hillsides and valleys was a prominent arch made of cut cedar trees and decorated with trims. The disciples all felt very much a part of this happy occasion and had obviously been very involved in preparation. Not only had they constructed the rustic arch, they disguised the ugly fire pit, made a dance floor area, set up chairs church style before the arch, and lots of ordinary cleaning and doing. Several disciples stood up with Trey attired in starched Levis and a white shirt. Music started and the procession started with bridesmaids in assorted bright color dresses. The little daughter was to be the flower girl but balked at the wrong time. So, she was carried down the aisle by a young man and handed to a grandmother. A beautiful bride in a soft, white, flowing gown proceeded on the arm of her father. She was glowing and Trey just beamed. Joshua officiated at the ceremony with his usual finesse and then offered the couple communion as a commitment to their union with Christ. It was the first wedding at the ridge and it was incredible.

After a wedding weekend together, Trey graduated from Oak Ridge the following Sunday with his wife and daughter at his side. They rented a house not many miles from the Ridge and quickly turned it into a home with the help of friends. Trey said that he wanted to stay close to the Ridge to ensure his commitment. We all prayed for his new life in Christ with a beautiful family. Time revealed that close proximity alone was not a guarantee of "making it" Keeping eyes on Christ and committing daily is a necessity. He yielded to his old habits and a family was destroyed. Friends of the Ridge helped his family gain stability, but no one can help a man who doesn't want help. Only time will tell if he, too, can face the challenge and defeat the demons." "Trust in the Lord with all your heart and lean not on your own understanding; in all your ways acknowledge him, and He will make your paths straight" (Prov. 3:5–6).

Who should marry? What is marriage? Why should people marry? Those questions are relevant only to the individuals involved and their Heavenly Father. God did not want for man to be alone as the Genesis story goes; and so, he created a helpmate, Eve, and blessed their union. Marriage is a sacred union between a man and a woman, two separate individuals become one in union with God. A Christian marriage is a commitment entered into for the glory of God. It's between the two individuals and God. It was never intended to be easy as nothing about human life is easy since the fall of man. But God is willing to bless, guide, and direct that marriage as long as couples invoke His presence with willing hearts. Time would tell if these Oak Ridge couples would continue to stay close to God, who loves them. Many are able to reconstruct marriages while others fail. Coming home is the beginning another growth opportunity for each man and woman.

THE OLD MAN SPEAKS WISDOM

It was a cold, wet, rainy Thursday and frankly, we were tired of the cold, wet, rainy days that January. Cold days depress me and I can just give thanks to God that I live in Georgetown, where we have very little winter. I'd been hunkered down in my little cottage on most of those dark days, not wanting to venture out into the bleak winter. Paul and I had been out quite a bit that week. So I was looking forward to an evening at home with Paul. We were listening to the news on TV and browsing Facebook when I came across Joshua's post about Testify that night. A disciple named Kurt would be testifying that evening preceding his upcoming Sunday graduation from the program. Kurt was a friendly guy — a real social butterfly of the group. I mentioned it to Paul and commented that our neighbor, Howard, had really taken a liking to Kurt.

"Howard will probably want to go out there, you know," I said to Paul. "Well, would you like me to call him to see if he wants to go with us?" asked Paul. I was feeling really torn inside. As much as I wanted to go, I hated the thought of being out in the blustery weather. When asked again, I replied, "Yes, call him. Kurt was the first disciple of the group that Howard met and I think he took a real liking to him. I have a pot of soup cooking that's big enough to share; we can take that." Sure enough, Howard was anxious to go and we were soon on our way to Testify at the Ridge.

Only a few people were there when we arrived. I had thoughts that I didn't have enough soup for all of us. Others must have thought the weather was foreboding, too, but my fear was allayed when cars began to arrive and the table was soon covered with food for all of us. Old acquaintances were catching up while new ones became acquainted. In the midst of the crowd were two new disciples who had arrived a day previous. Travis and Jay looked a bit shell-shocked with all the activity. They were so young! Both were responsive and willing to talk although one appeared quite shy. Later in the evening TJ would give me their contact information so I would be able to include their mothers in the Circle of Friends. I was very pleased to see the plan of support working.

After dinner we all settled in to hear Kurt's story. His mom and dad were present for his testimony. An 8x10 color photograph of Kurt circulated among the crowd. People grinned when they saw a much younger Kurt with a full head of carrot-red, kinky-curly hair. "My 'fro," he called it. He was all duded up in a white sport coat and looking very proud in the picture. Now he stood before us many years older with shortly clipped, graying hair, wearing jeans and a t-shirt. We sang Kurt's chosen song, "He Lives" with gusto and then his story began.

"I'm 52," he began. It was the story we'd heard before many times. He grew up in a small town with a loving, church-going family and no apparent reason to go astray. "I was just rebellious," he said. "I loved being the life of the party." It started with Granny's wine and sneaking beer, which progressed to pot, cocaine, and meth. "Rebellion took me away from church, God, and family values." He met his wife in a halfway program, and they got married in a shotgun wedding. He cycled in and out of that relationship and relationships with his two children with a series of highs and lows, good and bad. He was in and out of jail and prison and admitted to being arrogant, judgmental, and angry with a cold heart. "As I look back I see God working in every situation. He was waiting for me to look to Him, but I couldn't. I wasn't ready," Kurt said. "I finally found my rock bottom sitting in isolation in a jail cell after my third DWI. I began studying the Bible. The Old Testament especially spoke to me and the stories in Samuel really took on meaning. I would go to God and turn away over and over. I even tried to barter with God." He was finally able to cry out and felt God in his heart. The rebirth began. It wasn't long after that he came to Oak Ridge. I can identify with his last comment, "It's not about me. It's about Jesus."

Through his testimony I had listened with interest finding a common denominator between his and other disciple's stories. In my mind I kept wondering, "God, what am I to take away from this story? What is the lesson? What's unique?" Then it began to dawn on me as I looked around the room and into the faces of the other disciples. The key was his opening comment, "I'm 52 years old!"

To me, the disciples were "the boys." I saw them as "the boys" who were seeking a new life of faith and dependence on God. They were learning to live their lives in service to others as God directed. They were getting new highs from worship and prayer. They were spending time in God's Word rather than on the streets. They were making new friends who would hold them accountable. The old was becoming new and the dead were being reborn.

The Old Man Speaks Wisdom

"He's 52 years old! I get it, God." Kurt put it in words, too. There was a new group of disciples coming into the Ridge. Kurt was right, he was the old guy in the bunch. Well, in all fairness, there are still two other disciples who've seen the better side of 40. But that was the point. Like the two almost-twenty-year-old guys who arrived the day before, the latest crop of disciples were all very young. Kurt had lots and lots to teach these guys. If anything, he could say "Look at my choices and look where it got me. The better part of my life was wasted. Find Jesus! Find joy!" Praise God for that message. Bless Kurt for his testimony and the fine example of faith he displays.

Kurt graduated from the program and accepted a position on staff at Oak Ridge. Guys respect him and he is a diligent worker. He became friends with Carrie. Carrie often comes out there for Testify as well as being a leader in Celebrate Recovery. She is in charge of "The Landing" for teens at Celebrate Recovery. Anyway, they are both wonderful, Christian people who enjoy each other's company. It is so refreshing to see a friendship developing and moving carefully into the future together. Who knows what the future holds for them as a couple? But God didn't intend us to get into committed relationships quickly. There's just too much to discover about each other and true love must include God as a partner. It's a fine example for others in the program, too.

A CALL ON HIS LIFE

Time has a way of speeding forward before we realize it. Paul and I had not been out to the Ridge for Testify in about six weeks. Some had graduated and moved on, yet the beds were being filled with newly surrendered men. Over a short period of time new faces appeared and some mysteriously went away. Little is said about those departing, but bad choices sometimes lead to leaving or being asked to leave. There is a strict code of conduct and Joshua makes them toe the line. It has to be that way. Lives depend on it. We'd met a number of the new disciples at church and got to hug them and encourage them but we found that more and more we didn't have the intimacy of friendship that we get from sharing meals and worship together at the Ridge.

We decided to go to Testify one Thursday in October and invited our neighbors to go with us again. They expressed concern over impending thunderstorms and rain. They can be treacherous in Central Texas, but Paul is careful about risk and declared it safe to go. So off we went with a large pot of navy beans and ham to share. We discussed who would testify that night; we had never met him face to face. It was Ben, a returning disciple graduate, whom we'd seen on Facebook. Actually, my only knowledge of him was through Facebook where we'd befriended each other and shared posts like many disciples and friends do. It's just a great way to encourage and say we are praying for them.

Because of weather threats, the crowd was smaller, but the room was still full. I gazed around the room trying to find the speaker. I spotted him on the couch among a few brothers from the Ridge. He was slight of build and sported a beard. He was dressed casually in plaid shorts and a tank top. They seemed to be discussing his right upper arm which bore a large tattoo that appeared to be freshly done. It was new. I discovered that he had an inappropriate tattoo in that location and had recently had it covered with a very large ornate cross to reflect his new life and faith.

Each story begins in a different way and so did his tale. He had been raised in a loving family with a Christian background. Nothing in his picture perfect life could have predicted the choices he would make that ruined his life for a time. He attributes his exploration of drugs to seeking excitement and thrills. Once you go there you only want more and more. There is nothing you won't do to get the fix to maintain what you perceive as sanity and joy. And so alienation from family and a world of crime ensue. Arrest, warrants, and jail time are all a part of the devastating picture.

In that lifestyle, you have friends . . . of sorts. I wouldn't know what else to call them besides that or partners in crime. And, he had a very good one that was in the room that night. It was TJ! I'd never heard TJ's story of how he came to the Ridge or his surrender. Now it would be revealed through his friend Ben. We knew TJ as a very devoted member of the staff at Oak Ridge and an invaluable asset to Joshua and the disciples. He was soft spoken with kind eyes and a huge Christian heart. His faith is exemplary. And he certainly models the Christian life as Jesus taught it.

The man Ben described was not the TJ we'd come to know! We knew he had a checkered past in addiction; hence, he too had come here to surrender long ago. We didn't know what a prideful young man he'd been. Ben explained that TJ always had to lead and that wasn't good. He didn't take suggestions well and was very headstrong. Together they went down the paths of darkness of addiction and crime. Apparently TJ was still in jail when Ben was first given an opportunity to surrender to God at Oak Ridge. Like every other disciple the struggle was long, arduous, and painful, but it was worth it in the end with a totally changed life in Christ.

"I knew the way of Christ was the right and only way to be set free and gain the new life I now have with a family," he said. "I so wanted the same for my best friend, TJ. I knew his heart and his pride. I was fearful he wouldn't follow. He never had followed, always being the bold, unabashed leader. But I prayed and prayed."

Ben continued: "When TJ was released we got in touch with each other and I made my plea. He would struggle and fight all the way. He knew he wanted help and sought it in rehab facilities where he was kicked out." His story goes on to reveal his prayer after talking to TJ one night. TJ had just left one facility unsuccessfully and was on the way to more trouble. The room was quiet as Ben revealed what happened next. He had prayed to God telling him that anything short of killing TJ would have to take place, but he so wanted God to move and change his heart. God answered that prayer swiftly. While in route TJ was in a horrible accident. The EMS lost him; restarting his heart not once, but twice. It's almost unheard of for anyone to survive and become well after two heart events like this. But he did and he, too, came to Oak Ridge in surrender and found a new life in Christ.

Rain poured down the windows of the house at Oak Ridge as tears rolled down the cheeks of the listeners at Testify that night. Prayers of thanksgiving rose and joyful sounds of praise seemed inadequate. What a powerful testimony that was of two men. One man left an honorable world to seek excitement and trekked off into darkness only to find his way back to wholeness through our Savior. But, he never forgot a friend whose pride had led him on the dark path of addiction and crime. Only God could have touched him in such a profound way. God does love all of us and desires for all of us to hear the truth of salvation and be transformed through His grace.

Ben remembered we were friends on Facebook and released me to share his story because it might help someone else. He lives somewhere else in Texas with his wife and daughter. He obviously loves sharing his faith and has a big heart for the disciples.

Ben, TJ, and I had opportunity to speak shortly after the worship service. We all agreed that they had a story to share that may touch the lives of other people. So we agreed to sit down together at another time and place to be determined. However, the opportunity time was difficult to ascertain. One Wednesday after church service TJ came to me saying that Ben would be here this weekend and perhaps will have a chance to sit down and talk. Well, Saturday came and Ben was busy with his family, but I invited TJ to have lunch with me so we could talk. After lunch we settled into two recliners in the living room to chat. "Here's the part of the story I had already written after Ben's testimony," I said, while handing it to him. He read while I chatted with Justin who had come with him. Justin and TJ had run in a race to raise funds for a worthy cause that morning. It was TJ's day off and I was honored that he spent part of it with me. Justin, a current disciple in training said that he was anxious to hear this story, too. Justin, a young man with a broad smile and bright eyes, appeared to be a pitcher waiting to be filled. He was making good progress in his discipleship at the Ridge. I think it was an aunt and uncle who were his main support system. Later, he would go to live with them and pursue his education.

About that time TJ spoke, "One part is not quite the way it was." He went on to explain that he was just leaving prison in Chicago and on his way to a detox center. These guys know all the tricks and he was no different. He wasn't going to the detox center for help, but his intentions were to secure the drugs they give you. He said that he told them he was a heroine user but he wasn't. However, the drug they would give him to help him detox would give him the high he was seeking. TJ had called Ben and asked him to send money. Ben was hesitant, but after consulting Chester he sent forty dollars to TJ. Ben was fearful because he knew in his heart what TJ would do. However, Chester's words had been so wise and rang so true. "You can't deny him his rock bottom," Chester said. It's as if God spoke through Chester with those words. God wants to heal these guys, He loves them, but He needs for them to truly hit rock bottom to create a new man in Christ. And so, Ben prayed that God would turn TJ's heart to Him and save him. "Anything short of killing him," he prayed.

Of course, TJ did what you'd expect and spent the twenty dollars he had left on booze. "It was cold in Chicago, so I sought warmth in the public library. It was not very populated and was a good, warm place to be alone. I went into a stall in the bathroom to hide and consume my purchase." It was then, in a bathroom stall, hiding in a library that his heart stopped. TJ believes with all his heart that it was God that made that happen. With tears in eyes he told of many times he'd consumed hundreds of dollars' worth of drugs and alcohol with nothing similar happening to him. That night he had only twenty dollars! His heart stopped! He was totally broken and totally defenseless, but for the hand of God who did not desert him.

It's miraculous that someone found him right away and emergency vehicles were close enough to respond quickly. He was revived and his heart started. The emergency crew transported him to a hospital, but even that was not without drama beyond reason. His heart stopped a second time in the ambulance. The crew once again was able to reestablish a pulse and heartbeat. "God was there in his sovereignty," said TJ as we both reached for tissues. His doctor was emphatic that it was truly a miracle that he was alive as he recounted the events and the precise timing that had to be in place for TJ to live. People and emergency workers had been there in split seconds. The doctor told TJ it was difficult to get a heart to restart once it stopped, but twice was just amazing. He stated there was an eighty to ninety percent chance that they would not be successful in reviving him a second time.

For three to five days, he was in a coma and not reacting to any stimulus. Obviously, he came out of the coma, and God was at work in that too. No one seems to be able to explain how the hospital had his grandmother's phone number, but she was called. So, his brother came at grandma's request and through him their mother was contacted. "It was Mom's voice that brought me back to consciousness," TJ said. As his brother held the phone to his ear, Mom said, "Timmy, we miss you. We want you back." That's all it took. TJ opened his eyes to see his brother. Pride and embarrassment overtook him at that moment. TJ relates that he could remember the type of person he was though he couldn't remember most events from the previous year. It was then that Ben and Joshua offered him a bed at Oak Ridge and hope for recovery in Jesus.

"I couldn't get drinking out of my mind even though I know it had killed me." His brother hounded him as he wrestled his demons in frustration. He recounted his thoughts: "I don't understand. Jesus isn't for me. I know I need help. Can't I just get help without God?" You and I know the answer and he discovered it.

It was then that he reached out in desperation to Joshua. It was then that he pleaded, "God, if You're real, just show me." With apprehension and dread he came to the Ridge and it was still a struggle. He vividly remembers attending a church service with Oak Ridge guys as being a turning point. "It still gives me goose bumps," he said. "Every song and even the sermon, 'Don't Quit,' seemed to be directed at me. Conspiracy, I thought and even confronted the pastor." The pastor had smiled while telling him how the sermon was determined months prior as part of a plan for a year to reveal God's truth. He continued by saying, "I had no idea you'd be here or need that message today, but God did." TJ smiled as he recounted, "It was the first time I realized that God cared about me. That He believed in me!"

He came to realize that temptation comes from inside us: our sinful nature. We must fight the devil. God is the only power that can come against the evil inside us and in the world; he loves us and desires to be invited into our hearts. TJ's struggles were many, but Psalm 37:4 gave him hope: "Delight yourself in the Lord and He will give you the desires of your heart." He prayed, "God, make me a teacher."

This young man who presented himself to God at the lowest point of his life is now physically and spiritually made new through the grace of God. TJ graduated from the Ridge and went on staff helping others for several years. There was a disquieting episode after graduation, but my point is that he came back to the source of his strength: God. TJ felt God's call to the ministry and somehow had the assurance that God had a plan for that too.

He had a quest for knowledge and pursued it, but he too had to answer for outstanding warrants in Florida. He was incarcerated for months until he got his hearing. He testified to other prisoners during that time. His hearing finally came and charges were dismissed. As he returned to staff at Oak Ridge, he pursued his dream though there were many obstacles. He admits that it has all tried his patience and brought him to total reliance on God. And, I am so blessed to share with you that he has been accepted into seminary and leaves next week to continue his journey.

He has been in seminary for a year now, and I've kept in touch with him. I even had the pleasure of attending church with him in Fort Worth recently. Over lunch he told me how hard it had been for him financially during the first semester. He held two jobs plus being a full time student. He struggled and even thought of taking fewer classes the next semester because of physical and financial stress. "I just knew in my heart that God had called me to the ministry so I kept praying for guidance. Then, another miracle occurred. A scholarship was brought to his attention and he was accepted. The way to all the rest of his studies is paved with grace and payment in full. When you know you've had all you can stand, but kept your eyes on God, He makes your way clear.

WILD RIDE

Things back at home were still progressing as more men yielded to discipleship at Oak Ridge. I remember another evening that we'd gone to the Ridge for Testify. It was an entertaining evening. The end of the evening was approaching and Joshua asked the staff for reports and concerns. Then, with a sly grin and giggle he said, "Scottie, you and Chester tell about your ride back from Fort Worth." Joshua said we'd be able to see God moments all over this story. Scottie and Chester, a matched set of opposites, took center front. Chester started telling how they were on the way back from Fort Worth with David, a current disciple. David had been to a mandated court appearance accompanied by Chester and Scottie as representatives of Oak Ridge. David jumped in to explain how a day of dread ended up better than expected when he wasn't held accountable to penance for his crimes. A lawyer near them was amazed and commented that this judge never does that.

The guys grinned, knowing that it has happened before for those who change their hearts and mend their ways. That's a God thing.

They started home; Chester explained that he was only going 75 mph out in the country on the long, dark road home. Then, without warning, a huge, darting deer struck their windshield. The airbags deployed and their Suburban left the road, crashing into a high grassy area. It was unavoidable; there was no time to react. Chester explained that there had been a small sedan in the lane next to them and he couldn't swerve because it would endanger them, too. He was relieved that the deer had not hit the little car because it probably would have killed its passengers.

The guys jumped out as soon as the vehicle stopped and reached for cell phones. There was no signal. "We were going to handle it," said Chester, "but how?" They waved down a lone car passing by. Inside the car were a few country boys who'd been partying a bit too much. They were very verbal in their attempts to help and the words were less than acceptable to Christians, but help is help.

Scottie took over the story from this point at Chester's prompting. He was very dramatic in his portrayal, showing how he was standing just a few feet from the vehicle in the tall grass in total darkness when he heard a noise. He quickly recognized the distinctive sound of a rattlesnake. Screaming, he jumped away from the sound, obviously scared. The cowboys jumped into action to pursue the snake. This they accomplished by jumping in a vehicle and rolling forward and backwards in an attempt to run over the snake, shouting obscenities the whole time. The scene became more dramatic when Scottie realized his glasses had fallen off in that same grass as he made his escape. He yelled wildly for them to stop, but the cowboys persisted in crushing the snake.

Soon after, they stopped and retrieved a tool from their truck to decapitate the snake. All was well for the moment. Scottie and Chester bent over, searching the ground for the glasses. The headlights from the cowboys' truck gleamed at their backs; it was only then that the cowboys saw the Testify symbol of a praying man on the back of their shirts. As the cowboys sped off into the night, they rolled down a window and yelled back at the disciples, "God bless y'all!" The guys laughed and laughed. Disaster was averted and nothing was broken that couldn't be fixed. No one was hurt. The car will probably be totaled, but they were okay. It had been a very eventful day and God had truly shown up in a number of ways. Thank you, Father, for Your care and protection. Scottie even found his glasses unbroken.

It's good to laugh with friends, to really enjoy those moments in life which elude a drugged mind. It's good to find a new way to live and include God in it. You'll never find a better friend.

Another man came to the Ridge in a stupor. His life wasn't joyful or happy in any way when he was rescued from the streets. I'm told he was on his last legs when he arrived and in bad enough shape to be considered a life risk. The first time we saw Britt, he was pitiful. We got to know him over time and really watched God change him. As he began recovery, he started taking better care of himself and it began to show in his personal care, dress, and manners. Recently, I heard him relate a story about how much Brandon and other disciples had helped him grow and kept his spirits high. He really appreciated the kinship that developed. Eventually, he, too, would graduate. At that juncture Joshua offered Britt a staff position at the Ridge. His services were needed at the Ridge. He is not at all the same man we first met, thanks to God's intervention.

Something to know about Britt: he can put a meal together. He began helping in the kitchen with meals. It's a big task to make sure all those guys get three meals a day on a limited budget. He's made the most of the small kitchen and storage areas. Every month he announces an opportunity to contribute to the pantry by picking canned goods, or meat, or cleaning supplies or whatever is needed. They do have a budget which he has been able to cut significantly and still provide nutritious meals. That kitchen is run with precision as everyone takes a turn at helping. It's so neat to see Britt in charge. I can't even imagine the planning that goes into providing meals for such large numbers of hungry men — disciples and staff — for every meal. Compound that with the fact that you use what's in the pantry to be a creative cook, and you have a job that requires creativity, improvisation, budgeting, and organization. Not an easy task, but Britt handles the challenge very well.

TRIO OF TROUBLE

It was a cool night at Oak Ridge as we sat on the deck awaiting the testimony of a former disciple. Darkness was closing in over the hillsides and the only light visible was there on the deck. I couldn't help but think how God is the only light in a dark and hurting world. I smiled. It's always heartwarming to hear more stories of recovery in Christ. I didn't know this speaker or anything about him so it would be revealing. Brian, who had also been in the program, stepped to the mic to introduce his lifelong friend, Matt. They snickered like buddies as they called up Byron, a current disciple, who made it a trio of trouble. Brian explained that he had known Matt and Byron when they were young boys. He said, "We were knuckleheads growing up who could get in enough trouble to make a grown man cry." He shared many stories, each one worse than the previous one. But, at some point their focus changed and was no longer on how bad they could be. God had been good to these three musketeers.

After Brian proclaimed that Matt was truly a changed man and a role model who influenced him, Matt revealed his story. Matt spoke directly, "God's promises are coming true in my life. I'm a blessed man." He glanced over to his wife and family who were seated to my right. I could see tears in his wife's eyes as he continued his talk. "The devil can mess you up, but God's grace and blessings cover all of that and I've truly become a new creation in Christ."

His childhood had hints of similarities to other kids in today's world. There was alcoholism in the family and his parents had been focused on work, work, work. It allowed too much idle time to get into drugs, crime, and even the mafia. He explained, "I knew I had a disease. I couldn't walk away. I tried, but couldn't fix myself. I blew off football and college and allowed men to pull me deep into the drug world.

My thinking was crazy and I became so money hungry. I was deep in debt. I still don't understand fully why I'm a free man today. Another guy got a twenty-year prison sentence for grievances that were no worse than mine. I dodged bullets and prison and survived! I had an empty hole inside and had never been introduced to God."

"God had a plan for me if I would have just listened. He didn't give up on me. God put a godly woman in my life who could slow me down. There were times I put her through hell on earth. But she didn't give up and her faith was infallible." Sickness got his attention and he became still enough to listen. He started really hearing things he'd never heard before that can only be explained as God opportunities. Through his dad and a man named Richard, he became aware of Joshua's ministry. Oak Ridge had only been open about two months at that point in time.

"Are you ready?" his dad had asked. He told Matt about Oak Ridge saying, "It's a faith based program." "You mean God? I'm ready!" was Matt's reply. About midnight he would make a call to Joshua Harris and his own family. Joshua asked him what he wanted from the program. He replied, "I'm bringing you the devil and I just want Jesus. I'm broken and running from the devil as fast as I can. I'm a lifer with a disease." Matt had become one of the first disciples.

Looking at the disciples in residence he said, "This is the place where guys like you and me change. God will fill that empty hole inside and you will give your heart and life to him. God saves one life at a time." His life changed in big ways, but it took time. He had taken a year of living at the Transition House while continuing to grow in Christ and assimilate into his new life. In fact, it was three years before his wife would be ready to have him back home. Now he's giving God the place He deserves in his life and family. "I'm learning to help others and serve God." At that, his wife rose from her chair and went to him at the front of the group. As she hugged him there was evidence of a twinkle of respect and pride in her eye. God is good!

The third member of the trio of trouble was Byron. He was the third member of the group to come into discipleship at Oak Ridge. He can most ably be described a tall, lanky man with a boy's heart. I've never seen him without that sheepish grin. One night at church his stepmother came up to me to chat. She had been the trainer coach for a disabled student who worked for me at my boutique. It was a high school program that really helped kids with special needs and I was glad to take part. I knew this lady, Linda, only as the coach and the daughter of one of my long term employees, Ms. Betty. I'm sure I looked shocked when Linda told me she was Byron's mom. Wow! Small world, isn't it?

Paul and I got fairly well acquainted with Byron while he was at Oak Ridge. He always seemed pretty happy go lucky and was undaunted by the reality of life. He struggled with a relationship and tried to recover it, but I don't know that that happened. He, too, would graduate from Oak Ridge and would then choose to live at Transition House for a period of time.

That was a very good choice for him and I'm so glad it was available. Rumor has it that he is trying to get his journeyman electricians license now. Mom and Grandmother must be proud and thankful for the beautiful change in Byron's life.

IT'S A SMALL WORLD

The web of humanity is tightly woven and crosses many times. Many studies bear out the facts of our connection and relations to each other. No, I haven't changed topics nor have I diverted from my story. I only say this to reiterate the fact that our paths cross and our lives touch one another. I choose to believe that much of this connection is a God presented opportunity. Very few people with whom I've shared this story couldn't relate on some level to the realities of addiction in families and the damage it does. Some are motivated to service and offerings of support; while others use the information as a jumping off point for seeking help for someone they love. God brings us to the challenge and it's up to each person to accept or reject. I pray that seed fall on fertile ground.

Only recently we attended Spirit Fest, a Christian praise concert, with our extended Oak Ridge family. Jerry and Sharon had recently become involved with

Oak Ridge after going out there with us. They were joining us and brought along another friend, Linda. She knew little or nothing about the group. We're a very social, loving group and hugs are frequent. As I turned to hug a couple of disciples I was struck by the look on Linda's face. She really didn't know what to make of all of this. I just had that deep feeling that God was moving in this moment! So, I whispered a little prayer to my best friend, God. I feel sure that Linda talked about her feelings with Sharon, who related that Linda didn't know quite what this was all about. "I just really feel God wants me to be part of the support of this ministry and I don't know why." said Linda. That's just one of many examples of willing submission to God's direction. You never know where He will lead you, but you'll never go wrong following Him.

It's a network of opportunity that God creates for us to touch each other in ways that bring us to the full realization and acceptance of Christ as our Savior. God's message is for us to touch the lives of others, to witness to others, to live by example, and to give Him the glory. "This is good, and pleases God, our Savior, who wants all men to be saved and to come unto the knowledge of the truth" (1 Tim. 2:4).

The disciples themselves become strong and vibrant witnesses for the kingdom of God as they give their hearts to Jesus. When they graduate and go home they become God's witnesses and draw others to Him and healing. One shining example of God working through a graduate to extend His kingdom is Brent.

Brent, a sandy haired man of average size, came to the Ridge. But his quiet disposition made him almost invisible to guests and hard to get to know. He had kind eyes and would respond if you spoke to him, but he was difficult to engage in conversation. After the shock of arriving at the Ridge wore off, he became a reserved participant in the program. I have no knowledge about how he found this ministry from the far out edge of Texas, but he did. I can only assume that his story of addiction was as entangling as others that I'd heard. So, I don't know much about him personally except that he came from a small town in west Texas that was next to nowhere and almost as far. I don't even remember getting to know his wife or family well and they didn't come often because of distance. I watched from a distance as family members posted on Facebook, but that isn't really getting acquainted.

So, why is it important to share Brent's story? Well, it's a shining example of that web of humanity. Our lives touch others and if God's light shines through us, they want what we have. I have no doubt that a great deal of witnessing and praying went on for what would happen next. One night at the Ridge we met a new disciple, Sean. It was Brent's son. He was a mess when he arrived. Drugs had done extreme damage to him physically and emotionally, but, as with other disciples, the time came when Sean, too, became a new man in Christ. It's always so amazing to see the transformation from addicted soul to saved man. We went to the graduation the day that Sean completed the program. I am so proud that he stayed the course and won the prize. His dad, Brent, and mother, and wife attended the ceremony and gave the charge to Sean as Joshua directed. I wanted to see more exuberance, but that was not in Brent's nature. Just because we're not a "shout it from the roof tops" type of person doesn't mean we can't bring others to Christ. At the end of the graduation Joshua called up Sean's lady and they renewed their vows of commitment. Just think, a whole restored family is living God's way.

That alone would have been enough to share about disciples extending God's kingdom, but that witness then proceeded to extend into their community. Facebook posts demonstrated Brent participating actively in his home congregation. There were also posts about their eating establishment. We heard little on a personal level of Brent or his family until . . .

Arriving at church one Wednesday evening, I proceeded to the other side of the sanctuary from our usual seats. The boys know I'm coming to greet each of them with a hug and a word. Sometimes it's just a simple greeting and other time I let their faces guide me in what to ask them. Each of them needs encouragement and I love encouraging. Any new guy that comes gets a nudge from another disciple and a quick explanation, "That's Mama Kay."

The greeting was going well and we were conversing as I moved from guy to guy swiftly. As I went to the other side of the group I became aware of a new man sitting at the front. His head was down and his shoulders drooped. His arms were crossed as if he were closing himself off from everyone and seeking isolation. That's not a good sign. So, I made a point to go near him and speak to him. I didn't know him; he was a recent arrival. My heart just kept telling me to try to get him to engage. After a few questions and statements his short, quick answers became longer. Then, he offered more without urging. He was struggling, but knew he was in the right place at the Ridge. He seemed fearful that he would not be able stay the course. "When I feel this way, I isolate myself." he said. A couple of other disciples stood near and began to add to the conversation. They seemed surprised he was talking, saying he'd been that way for several days. God can reach anyone — even in the depths of ourselves.

James and I developed a bond that evening. I really enjoy talking to this tall, young man with the slicked-back hair. He has come out of his shell and is very forthright in his story telling. He's on his way to a life in Christ. During one of several meals we've shared together at the Ridge, he told us how he came to be there. You could have knocked me over with a feather. He is from that same small never heard of town in far west Texas where Brent and his family live. "Yes, I know Brent and a lot of others from Denver City. I live there. I go to the same church." Are you beginning to see this tapestry of life spreading into a community? It's amazing! We have enjoyed getting to know James and encouraging him. I think he's going to make it! I found hope in his darkness.

A few weeks after we met James we met another new man. His name is Rico, and guess where he's from? It's Denver City, about as far away as you can get from here and still be in Texas. Oh, yes, he knows Brent and James. In fact, they have both told us how they were brothers on the street and in addiction. James seems to feel comforted that he knows Rico and has him here. I've cautioned them each to work their own plan individually and support each other in the fight. Misery loves company and I can only pray they don't find it in each other. God has a plan and it is being revealed.

THE SEARCH FOR SELF

*S*ometimes it takes years of being lost and searching before Jesus becomes the answer. He is always there patiently waiting. I mentioned the other older disciples in the room as Kurt testified. One of them, Robert, will be important later in this story. Well, in truth he wasn't much older than Kurt and was definitely much younger than me. My eyes fell on him as I thought about so many young disciples in the room. Robert was not young. His hair was gray and long, but pulled back in a rubber band at the nape of his neck. He had an exaggerated moustache, too. Like Kurt, Robert was tall and thin. At first, he wasn't very outgoing and we didn't get to know him well until later in the program. Like other disciples, given time his personality would bloom as he grew in his relationship with Christ.

Earlier in my writing I described the day the disciples came to help with my yard rejuvenation in the spring. Robert was one of those disciples that worked in my yard that day. In fact, he ran circles around the younger guys. Oh, not literally, but he had a method to his work and a strong work ethic. I appreciated his willingness to do any task and to clarify for sure what I wanted. He kept busy moving stones, digging up beds and enlarging them, as well as other tasks. In fact, he was the one that noticed they hadn't finished the gutter cleanout while we were eating. He quickly finished his meal and while others relaxed, he grabbed a ladder and finished the job. Josh had just been telling me of Robert's integrity. He was right. He was concerned that Robert would be graduating soon and it was not in his best interest to go back to North Carolina.

Earlier in the morning, I asked Robert about his family. He took a few moments to tell me about his children. They now lived with their mother, his ex-wife. He was very complimentary about her mothering skills and the friends they had become. He began to tell me about the kids. Tears fell as he told me about his daughter, who has a type of autism. His love and concern was so obvious in his expression that it touched my heart. I had an affinity with him in that moment. I held a master's degree in special education and had specifically loved teaching autistic children. They are almost always very bright; we just have to find a way to help them reach their potential. I sent my DVD movie of "Temple Grandin" with him hoping it would help

The Search For Self

him better understand his daughter. Temple Grandin is about an autistic adult with an amazing career and is an advocate for others. Many months later I would have the opportunity to introduce him to a young lady I had known many years. I was her teacher advocate when she was four years old. At that time her prognosis was not good and she had many learning difficulties including learning as an autistic child. I had reconnected with her when she became my student helper in our church camp. I now introduced her to Robert saying that she was a senior in high school who had helped me in camp. She was poised and spoke politely. After she left, I looked at Robert and said, "That can be your daughter in the future. She's autistic and has struggled to become who she is now." Robert's jaw dropped. He had just gained new hope for his daughter. It was just a little God wink opportunity that blessed someone. I always look for opportunities to bless others.

Robert graduated the same day as Cody, the young sprite. Cody's family was all there beaming at his change and celebrating with him. They also accepted Joshua's charge to hold him accountable. There was Robert on the stage with only David to stand with him. He received cards from his children which brought tears, but none of his family came. "I've let them down so many times," he said. I poked Paul as I stood saying, "Come on. He needs family and I nominate us." Paul and I stood with him that day as his family and accepted the charge from Joshua. We were so proud of the new man he'd become.

He worked for a time at the Ridge. He had developed a real heart for ministry and found great joy in being an encourager. He had an empathetic ear for the disciples. He had taken the position partly because he knew he could never go home to live his new way of life. It wasn't long before he chose to leave the Ridge and establish a life in Georgetown close to new friends. After persistently looking for work and trying a few jobs, he landed a very good job with benefits. He's so happy and sees a bright future since he discovered that he truly is a child of God.

One day Robert had an opportunity to tell me how he came to Oak Ridge. He had lived in North Carolina and had a serious addiction problem. His life was a total disaster thanks to his addictions to alcohol. He described himself as a wild child who was totally self-centered back in the seventies and eighties. His mother had serious health issues, but his dad had seen he went to church. "I prayed that God would protect me and not kill me, but I wasn't willing to change. I destroyed relationships with several godly women who came into my life because I was so focused on myself. I'd been in detox five times and failed in all of them. Fortunately, I met my friend David from Texas in one of them. It was David whom I finally called for help," declared Robert. On a Monday he was released from a VA detox center and by Wednesday, drugged with Lithium pills from detox, he boarded a bus to Texas. He was on the bus from Wednesday to Friday but it's all a blur. He couldn't tolerate eating food. He stepped off the bus at seven in the morning and was met by his friend David. They arrived at Oak Ridge by two that afternoon but he still had a serious drug overhang. He vaguely remembers from his stupor the road to Oak Ridge thinking, "Where does this road end? I remember passing old trailers and goats and rickety fences and again wondered where in the world this was," Robert grinned. "At that point all that went through my mind was 'What have I done?' and then I saw the open gate, the good house, and the guys who seemed warm and friendly." Then, he went on to describe other programs in which he'd been and how Oak Ridge seemed at first like a day camp to him. Then it became real as he began to work the program. He reflected, "If they do what they say, it's what I want. I wasn't afraid of hard work and doing my part. I was so blessed to be in this discipleship. God became very real to me there and I could really give my life to Him."

THE SPRITE

The sprite I refer to now is the same free spirited young disciple I wrote about in the story about the disciples in my garden. Cody was so full of himself and impulsive. He seemed to be hung somewhere between boy and man. Whatever he focused on demanded his full attention. Sad to say that often meant he was hot or cold in his Christian walk. He made me think so much about my own son, Cody, who died making a bad choice.

Cody had graduated from the Ridge at the same time as Robert. He gave his testimony that Sunday morning in Life Group at church and his family was there to celebrate with him. Pride and hope filled their eyes as they attentively listened to his story. His father spoke briefly about the change in his son. It seemed unbelievable that this boy they had to stop helping was this same young man today. Cody seemed and professed to be on fire with the Holy Spirit and was sure

The Sprite

he could overcome his past through Christ. But when you become so self-assured you open an opportunity for the devil to influence you. And so it happened.

Cody didn't last long at the Transition House because he succumbed to temptation of drugs. It was the Fourth of July and we were in the park having a picnic with Julie and Bronson. Shortly before the skies darkened we were joined by some graduates from the Ridge who had come to enjoy the fireworks. Cody was with them, and boy, was he full of himself. He was Mr. Hyper Energy as he flitted about and wandered away and back to the group. Something was off and I sensed it but I couldn't put my finger on the problem. I challenged him lovingly, but he blurted out a quick reply that I can't forget. "I'm a man," he pronounced. "I can make my own decisions." Warning signs were evident, but not to him. That's just the way the great deceiver, Satan, works. That was the night he fell. He couldn't seem to give up his old contacts and refused to reset his phone. Why do we set ourselves up for failure? I've done it myself and it's not easy to live in a free choice world. Joshua and the disciples all reached out to Cody. Joshua offered him help and a way out. But Cody thought he knew best. He lied and deceived and took advantage of friends. He flip-flopped over and over between choosing God and choosing the world. It was hard to watch. We all kept praying.

I need to divert to my own story at this point. It was through Carrie and other friends that I became increasingly aware of the Celebrate Recovery program offered at First Baptist Church. Over the years I had been aware of other people who had sought personal growth and change through this program, but I was not impressed that it was something I needed to do. After all, I had been working on becoming a better me all my life. I had been a compulsive eater and used food to comfort for years in my life and at one time had weighed 340 pounds at the highest. I had dieted successfully over and over to lose great amounts of weight only to regain it. I thought I had overcome those compulsive feelings, but once in a while it rears its ugly head. I tried to explain this to Paul one night. He had commented that he just didn't understand why you would eat compulsively or make bad food choices when it made you feel ill. That was his reaction to an episode I'd just endured which resulted in illness. I tried my best to explain how it was really no different than the addiction our disciples experienced. It's a search for feeling good and protecting yourself and killing your pain. If I overeat I become numb to the fears and anxieties and pain that I perceive. "I can totally identify with them at the peak of self soothing. You know in your heart it's wrong and won't help to fix your hurts with food, alcohol, or drugs. The only trouble with that is that nothing can fill that

The Sprite

hole but God." Addiction is anything that takes your eyes off God and holds you in its snare.

I also became increasingly aware that I'd been co-dependent for years and yielding to it. Until you discover the source of your pain and deal with it, you'll keep on trying to fix yourself. Carrie and I talked often about my struggles and she encouraged me to go to Celebrate Recovery. I had become acquainted with Carrie at the Ridge. I, also, knew that the disciples attended Celebrate Recovery every week and completed a step study as part of the program.

At first, I went for someone else. I went to be a support for my friends. But I quickly realized that I had my own battles to fight with hurts, hang-ups, and habits. I needed to go deep in my study and enlist God's support and guidance. Celebrate Recovery is an incredible program for Christian recovery that started at Saddleback Church in California and is now nationwide. Like AA, it protects anonymity and steps for recovery. Unlike AA, it is Christ centered. There are lessons, testimonies, prayers, praises and sharing in groups. Not many people realize the program is for more than alcoholics and drug addicts, but it is! I would recommend it to others with any hurts, hang-ups, or habits.

So, I know you've got to be wondering how this all relates to Cody. By the way, I have permission to use his name and experience as well as Carrie's to explain how God works through Celebrate Recovery. Well, hold onto your seat because this is the point at which God blew my mind again. I had been going to Celebrate Recovery here for months and had even begun a step study. Several weeks it was not convenient to attend the local meeting so I sought out another church that offered the program on a different night and went there several times a month.

One night I went to Celebrate Recovery at that church about a thirty-minute drive from home. It was on that occasion that something amazing happened. I'd gone to large gathering as usual and enjoyed the testimony and lesson presented. I always loved singing with the praise band, too. Then, we broke to go to small group sharing. It's a large, large church facility and I had met only a few people there. For some reason as I crossed the lobby I got a funny feeling that God wanted my attention, but I didn't understand what He seemed to be sharing with me or why. But I was obedient to His will. He had asked me to just sit in the lobby and not go to sharing. It didn't make sense at all; however, I complied because God seemed so insistent. So I found a cozy, leather chair at the far side of the big lobby and just sat. No one else was there. "Now what?" I thought. "I have no book to read, no phone or electronic device so what shall I do for an hour?"

The Sprite

"Okay, God, what's this about?" I didn't have to wait long. Out of the corner of my eye I caught view of a man rushing across the lobby toward the elevator. His back was toward me but he seemed strangely familiar. "Cody?" I queried as he pushed the elevator button. He wheeled around in disbelief and shock. "Mama Kay, is that you? What are you doing here?" I smiled as he came strolling over to join me. "This has to be one of those God moments," he said, shaking his head. It still seemed so unreal to both of us. "You never know when God is going to show up or how. But He loves you and so do I," I replied.

Cody settled into the comfy chair facing me and we had a wonderful hour conversing. He wanted to know why I was there and I told him all of it. "I think God sent you here at this moment," he said. I agreed; he began to share the rest of his story.

He had been homeless and wandering the streets in Austin. Drugs had taken hold again along with all that goes with it. Because of his choices he was no longer welcome at home either. His family had made the commitment to not enable him anymore. Cody is smart. He had sound teaching. He knew he was wrong. But he couldn't seem to sustain his new life in Christ. That happens when you have old wounds that haven't completely healed. Through a stranger on the streets he got help. He had just gotten out of a "cold turkey" detox, in a facility. I'm still not certain if he walked all the way to Cedar Park from downtown Austin or if he took a bus part of the way. The important thing is that he had "made a bee line" to Celebrate Recovery at his home church. I had no idea it was his home church.

We talked for an hour and intermittently he tried to reach his family by phone. It was a good talk about what he needed to do now. Well, my co-dependence reared its ugly head, but I resisted. I did take him to a hamburger place to get him a meal. He still hadn't reached anyone about a place to go. I questioned him intently to make sure he was safe in this environment. "I'm a survivor," he said, "and this is a safe neighborhood. I live a few blocks from here. I'll be okay." And so, I left him there, praying he would make it this time with God's help.

The next morning, I got a call from Cody; he was so excited. "God showed up again," he said. He went on to explain how he'd been asleep in a park near his house when his dog woke him up by licking his face. Apparently a family member had let the dog out of the house during the night. He said that he took the dog home and knocked on the door. It was that knock that brought his father to the door. He stepped out to talk and after a while he allowed Cody in the house. "I'm home," he said.

Well, it's been a few up and downs since that day, but I think there is hope for Cody. He's no longer at home,

The Sprite

but he is working. He is trying. I found out that he is currently going to a Celebrate Recovery step study and that is good. In a testimony given at Celebrate Recovery I heard something that really hits the mark here. The man said, "I had to see the deception of my life style. I had to admit that I was being deceived by myself and others. I had to allow the Word of God to transform me instead of me conforming to God's will." If he can let God take charge of his life, he will make it. I guess that goes for all of us. It's all about God being central in our lives and living to fulfill His purpose for us. Amen! "Be still and know that I am God." Psalm 46:10

SHAW'S TRANSFORMATION

As I was writing one of the last stories that would be included in this book, God put someone on my heart. I was really focused on completing the story that I felt was to be the last one included. However, I think God had other ideas because my mind kept returning to a graduate from years before. We'd become acquainted with Shaw when he was a disciple at Oak Ridge. We really didn't get to know him well or hear his story. He had graduated and I believe he was one of the first graduates to live in the Transition House that was recently acquired by the ministry. He continued to come out to Testify as he made his transition into the real world. Connection with the brothers is so important at this stage of recovery.

We heard that he had moved to Austin and was doing well. He took a position at some kind of half-way house as supervisor and was also doing some carpentry work. He and others helped with Church Under the

Bridge in Austin. As I understand it, this place is located under the expressway in downtown Austin and is very near the central police station. That seemed ironic, but it's where homeless people gather for safety and shelter. People from Oak Ridge, churches, and Gideons come to minister to these people. They share what is needed: supplies, food, and the message of salvation.

I followed the urgings of my heart to somehow include Shaw in the story. I really had a feeling that God had placed something I needed to share in his heart. So, I made a few calls to establish contact and then had a very meaningful visit with Shaw on the phone. Several details of his story really brought a message of truth and clarified my understanding.

His first point was, "Until you're finished, you're not done. You have to be truly broken." Jesus is waiting for that opportunity. He asked me if I'd seen a movie about the crucifixion of Christ. "There were prostitutes in the sand grasping and crawling to Jesus at the cross. That's how desperate one must feel to be able to receive new life in Christ. I was so very sick and broken when I got to Oak Ridge." He crawled away from a homeless, pitiful life to the waiting arms of God's helpers. He reflected how difficult the process had been and the depths of the emotions experienced.

Shaw had a very ugly past involving drugs, alcohol, sexual sin—almost any evil thing a person can experience. He'd had lots of warrants, foiled lots of bail bondmen, skipped on many legal issues and responsibilities. Because we're human, the opportunities to sin are always there. He was trapped, but on his way to new life.

"I died to myself right there on the mountain," he said. "Jesus changed my life at the Ridge." He is first to thank Joshua for his coaching and persistence. On and on he goes about the absolutely blessed opportunity that is given to these disciples through the Oak Ridge ministry. "Joshua is tough, he understands, he knows the way, and he cares. Joshua is a shepherd." That speaks volumes about Joshua Harris, Oak Ridge, and the Transition House.

He would also want you to know that the Transition House was huge in making his way to a new way of life. "You have to get it," Shaw says. The Ridge owns a white rock home on a cul-de-sac in a Georgetown neighborhood. Graduates are afforded an opportunity to live in that house with brothers during a period of transition. Accountability is required. It gives them time to get on their own feet while being held accountable by their fellow residents. Mike currently oversees that home and each resident participates with a monthly fee. Shaw and others have emphasized over and over the importance of reentering life with support of the Transition House. It's been a blessing.

Shaw asked us to come to the Ridge to hear his testimony the next Thursday. We went. We heard. We were astounded again by his testimony and truths. I love his comment, "Don't put God in a box. You can't do that. You only box yourself." God is all powerful. He can move mountains and do the unbelievable because of His great love. Shaw's final message was an admonition. Stay in connection. Stay plugged in. Stay connected to the church. Continue to develop a personal relationship with God.

The Transition House is a success in helping to write the rest of the Oak Ridge story. I thank God for Joshua and the board of Oak Ridge seeing this need and providing this opportunity to graduates.

A number of men have availed themselves of this opportunity to grow in independence. Being a wage earner is absolutely necessary to the new life. It's time to pull yourself up by your boot straps and get on with providing for yourself.

One of the guys who went through the Ridge and lived at the Transition House is named Troy. Troy is quiet and seemed introverted while at the Ridge, but I sometimes pulled up a seat next to him and engaged him in conversation. His words are wise and so deep. He had committed many verses of scripture to memory. He could reflect with understanding Bible stories. I really enjoyed his company. He is a big man with a gentle heart. I loved hearing him speak at graduation ceremonies. He had a wonderful way with words. Troy graduated and moved into the Transition House for a time. He was gainfully employed as an electrician and traveled some. Later, he would move into an apartment and finally home.

Troy is an inspiration to his brother, Cristian. You couldn't help but tell they were brothers. They looked just alike. Their imposing size and gentle spirits made them memorable. Cristian loved and respected his brother. So, Cristian, too, would become an Oak Ridge disciple and upon completion of the program would go to the Transition House. Cristian took over Mike's position of leadership at Transition House when Mike left to reunite his family. Our friends, Jerry and Sharon, offered Cristian the opportunity to become a desk clerk at their hotel. We pray Godspeed for these men and for all involved in Oak Ridge.

NEVER OUT OF SATAN'S REACH

There are often men who come to the Ridge that have the same first name as previous participants. So it was when we met a second Brandon, Brandon Buddy. Brandon Buddy didn't appear to be more than an ordinary guy. But there were some surprises in store. It wasn't until it was nearly time for his graduation that we became aware of his whole story.

"I was not rescued to give me life but to give life to others. I want to reach the ones that need help. There are millions of lost souls and God has called me to make a difference." That's how Brandon Buddy started his story as he found a comfy chair in my living room. He gave me permission to use his whole name as he thought a reader might recognize it or find it on the web to give credence to his story. You will come to realize that no one is exempt from the wiles of Satan, not even those in the public eye.

I had so looked forward to the time he could share his testimony. With furrowed brow and pensive expression Brandon went on to carefully and thoughtfully clarify his thoughts. "Now, I wasn't called to preach. I just want to carefully share God's story with lost souls and present to them the plan for salvation. God makes the difference. There are millions of lost souls for whom God yearns. Just want to be my authentic self."

Paul and I had come to know Brandon at the Ridge and church services. He was tall and handsome, and had almost black wavy hair and dark, deep eyes. He always seemed quite introverted in comparison to the other guys. Although he always had a receptive smile and visited cordially when approached. He was a mystery and we knew nothing of his story.

Graduation came and he was to testify on Thursday. I really regretted that we had a conflicting event and wouldn't hear it. Joshua put out a teaser in the invitation to Testify that really peaked my interest. I had no idea who Brandon really was and wanted more of his story. It was definitely unique. His authentic self would be shared that night, but I was privileged to hear it as he accepted my invitation to visit one day.

"I was always a believer, though I wasn't churched," Brandon started, "Mom taught us about God and how

Jesus died so we can live. I can't remember when I didn't know that. And I learned to talk to God. Pray."

The parts of the story about his growing up bore similarities to other disciples with some points of difference. His parents divorced and he had a stepfather. He'd been successful at sports and finished high school in the top ten to fifteen percent of his class. This was in spite of the fact that the family moved frequently throughout those years, which made it very difficult to form any friendships that lasted. "My sister and I became best friends and still are," he said, glancing across the room at his sister, Kristen. She confirmed how close they were and how grateful she was to have her brother and best friend back. There had been separation between them during the time when he had spun into the depths of addiction. Their common bond and friendship had been restored and it was so obvious to see in their glowing faces.

The story continued with the family's move back to Austin, where they worked in the hospitality industry. Brandon was open to options and so attended a job scouting event one day. He visited with recruiters but recalls one specifically. "Did you ever want to act?" the recruiter asked. It took Brandon totally by surprise but somehow he was led to think about it and pursue. "Out of the whole process I only got one call back, but it was the right one," smirked Brandon. It was from the man who had inquired about him wanting to act! After much thought Brandon finally agreed to move to Los Angeles at age nineteen to strike out on his own in an acting career. There was no party scene, no clubbing; just hard work as he tried to establish himself. His future wasn't looking good as he went on up to twelve auditions in one week. He felt his manager wasn't really supporting his efforts, but he was swayed by the clients for whom Brandon auditioned. Brandon related that at least half of the twelve called the manager back saying, "Don't send another one like this. He'll never work."

Still, Brandon remained undaunted and determined to continue his pursuit. "I really talked a lot to Jesus. I prayed and prayed." He said he started to read trade books and study acting. It was only then that he realized there was more to it and became infatuated with the craft. He got an acting job! He played a role in the pilot of a series, "A Hero's Welcome" for network TV. The series didn't make it, but that was okay because of what followed. His manager called him to go to New York to read for a network soap opera part. He'd read for this same part earlier but this was the callback of finalists. Brandon got the idea that his manager didn't anticipate success when he told him to just enjoy the free trip to New York. After all, there were three thousand applicants for the part. There were a number of other guys on the same plane that were destined for the same tryout. "I could spot them," he said. "We all looked alike." Then, he laughed and explained more. Sure enough, all ten of those guys had the opportunity to test with the actress. The others exited the film test self-assured that they personally had been selected. Brandon didn't know what to think, but a week later he had his answer. Brandon Buddy played this character on the network soap opera for four years after surviving thirteen weeks on a probationary contract.

It was a new life and an exciting time for Brandon. He was so excited, but he didn't want the superficial excitement of a famous, fake life. "I really tried hard not to become the stereotypical actor," he said. Reality set in as he became absorbed in his new lifestyle. He reached a level of that life where he saw the dark side of humanity. People's actions were appalling and they lived in a surrealistic world. His sister added that he is so sensitive that he really internalized all of it. He began to lose touch with his ability to discern between the realities. After two years of fame as the soap character, he lost contact with Jesus and became totally absorbed by worldly living. He would live about two more years in this surreal existence. "It was all about me in the chaotic world where social drinking turned to a daily necessity," he reminisced. He became unable to function without alcohol and found steroids enhanced his ability to act. "I had no authentic self as I strove to be to the person everyone wanted me to be. It was pretend. I didn't know me anymore. I was totally immersed in wild living and show people and drugs and alcohol."

After about four years he'd had enough and returned to Austin as a very addicted person. He tried to hide the drinking from family, but they saw pretty quickly that those bottles weren't full of water. It was then that he experienced his first seizure and EMS was called. Xanax was prescribed by a psychiatrist to allay his fears of seizing again. He returned to work in New York, but network executives and soap opera directors quickly saw the deterioration. They attempted to sweep it under a rug. He met his goal of never walking off set and finished his contract in spite of being a mess.

He returned home to Austin, avoiding legal issues in New York. His manager urged him to get back to Los Angeles, seeing Brandon was a hot commodity, but Brandon crumbled right away. "I was so far gone that Jesus wasn't even given a second thought," he commented. "The devil foiled any plans to recover with seizures, withdrawal, blackouts, family rejections, and homelessness. I stayed in hotels as long as I had money and then slept in my car. Cops were always running me off." He was even jailed and hospitalized, but quickly released as no agency wanted to assume responsibility for what was perceived as imminent death. Consequently, he ended up sleeping in a

Georgetown park until he called his mom to come get him. She was on her way, but he started walking down the expressway in the direction of home. He said that several concerned citizens called 911 reporting "a dead man walking."

Firetrucks and EMS reached him just as his mother appeared on the scene. This is the point in the story where God became very evident in the picture. The opportunity to return to God came through a Georgetown fireman named Brad, who first attended Brandon. As Brandon was loaded for transport he says that fireman went to his mother. It was fireman Brad who shared Oak Ridge Disciple House and other options with her.

"The only thing I hadn't tried was Jesus," he explained as he told how his mother and sister had pleaded with him to let Jesus in and offered him the opportunity to go to this Christian based disciple house. It was in January 2015 that he was accepted for the open bed at Oak Ridge. He was willing to listen and accept help, but it wasn't without a "foxhole prayer." He grinned, "You know, the one where you tell God, 'just save me now and I won't do it again.'" He referred to Oak Ridge as "a blessed opportunity for each man to check out of society for six months to be with God on the mountain. I learned how to pray and learned to listen for His response. I came to know God and Jesus and understand more about Him. Through this I began a personal relationship with him and it felt good. Jesus really loves me but He allows lessons to help me grow. I really value my relationship with God and know He loves me. For so long I'd stare in the mirror trying desperately to recognize me in that soulless reflection. Now I see me, a redeemed child of God!"

He had a plan to return to acting eventually, but first he would live and work in Austin for a time. His managers were working for him and he was working on himself to refresh skills and rejuvenate health wise. He had legal obligations to reconcile. He had a future, though the details weren't clear yet. "God saved me to give life to others. Isn't that God's plan?"

That, in a nutshell, is God's plan. God loves us, saves us, and extends grace to us — all to fulfill our purpose of living lives that glorify God and bless others.

Paul and I had made a point to attend the graduation of Sean and Brandon. It was held at a local mortuary, which is the usual venue. They happily allow the ministry to use their chapel for the ceremony. We had found it curious when we first attended graduations, but quickly came to realize the significance of the place. These men are symbolizing burying of their old man and becoming new creations in Christ.

Joshua opened with his message. The disciples each gave their charge to the graduate after hymns were sung. Next came the ceremony of gravestones and commitment. Sean was surrounded by family. His proud father, also a graduate, was beaming. Brandon was joined by his brother-in-law as his mother and sister were in California. It was then that Joshua invited another man forward. It was Brad, the fireman who had attended to Brandon and referred his mother to Oak Ridge. Tears came to my eyes. Why are we always so amazed when we see examples of God using his people to touch the lives of others? This was the link that brought Brandon back to God. We should all look for the opportunities that God presents us and pray that we become more aware of his persuasion.

GOD DIRECTS OUR PATHS

God directs our paths; that's evident. It is never the same path for each individual. The common thread is God. I am reminded of how we are all part of God's amazing tapestry He's weaving. Threads of many different people, attributes, and histories form colorful stories of life. Yet, our paths cross as the tapestry is woven. Some threads break and are mended. Some break and never continue. Still others are stronger as they're woven and the tapestry takes on God's intention. The strong ones become the core of God's work while others fill a supporting role also necessary to the body and design of the quilt. They tend to harmonize in color raising praise to their Creator. God has many tapestries and quilts, but the Oak Ridge tapestry is the one dearest to my heart. I love to close my eyes and visualize this tapestry of God's creation blanketing the world in a rainbow of colors and facets.

And so, I know in my heart that God is now creating an additional tapestry or two. I sincerely pray that this is with Joshua's blessing, too. Joshua has a huge job assigned by God with the ministry at Oak Ridge. It is truly a remarkable and successful program boasting an extremely high success rate in recovery. Joshua protects the program and rightfully so. There is more to do for God's kingdom, but he needs to focus on that special ministry. God has callings for all of us. Have you heard yours?

One new tapestry is the Circle of Friends, the women's ministry, which I am blessed to lead. I inserted the story of the circle earlier in the book, but now it continues to grow and flourish doing God's work. Joshua saw this as God's plan and encouraged me to strike out independently. As a consequence, God has brought together the most amazing, unlikely group of women. Some of the ladies who are mothers and wives of disciples continue and are joined by Celebrate Recovery gals. We have an unlikely group from proper church ladies, professional women, recovered alcoholics or drug users, mothers, daughters, single, married, and on and on. But you know what? We've each discovered that we're created in God's image and He loves each of us. We've found we have lots in common; it's beautiful. We meet on Wednesday for Bible study and are currently working our way through *Becoming Myself* by

Stasi Eldredge. There are currently twenty-three on roll but some participate from afar. So there's usually seven to fourteen of us that gather regularly.

Just this week we celebrated the completion of our first study with a ceremony that was heartfelt. After opening with prayer in a circle around my table, we lit candles to acknowledge God's presence that we prayed would continue to bless us. I shared selections from Ransomed Heart Ministries blog that I printed from the website. In between each reading we completed a task. We shared fruit and juice, as we acknowledged our desire to live lives in which the fruits of the spirit were evident. Because we spent a lot of time in the study on revisiting our lives to date, including our hurts, we took meditation time with God to reflect on our past. Given a daisy, each lady was asked to release her hurts one by one, pulling a petal from the flower to symbolize each hurt. They seemed to take the task seriously as petals began to fall. We shared our group song, "Circle of Friends" and committed to further friendship. Each of my friends was given a rosebud as a symbol of blooming in God's garden and growing in faith. These women have blessed me and helped me grow in Christ.

The second is a newly formed group that supports graduates and their families as they transition into the real world from the Ridge. Currently, we just refer to them Guys in God's Service. The need was there and seen by a number of people who love and support Oak Ridge. Several guys are stepping up the efforts to extend God's love to others guys who struggle. It only lacked organization and a team. Robert, the graduate I wrote of earlier, was first to answer God's call. In talking with him since leaving the Ridge we came to know his heart better. He really wants to bless, and lead, and teach other guys who have fallen. About the same time, a man named Bronson was searching for other ways to help these men. Bronson and Julie are faithful supporters of Oak Ridge and in addition, hire many graduates to work in their company. Bronson really feels they are given all the tools for life during their stay at the Ridge as they develop relationships with God, but they need a boost to re-enter life. Upon graduation they have immediate needs for housing, jobs, restoring family relationships, and just walking the walk of life

Both these guys became very proactive in reaching out to graduates who needed more. They were there. They needed a team of prayer partners and supporters and resources. So it was that Paul and I invited friends to Thanksgiving dinner one Friday in September. No, it's not Thanksgiving, but we have so much to be thankful for and we needed to gather in community for prayer. I roasted a stuffed turkey and other families brought accompanying dishes. It was a great evening. After dinner and apple pie from Alicia, we gathered to pray and discuss. We discussed the success of Oak Ridge, its value, and how much we all want to continue to support that. But there's more to do for the graduates and their families. We need to extend God's message of love to them as a separate group. Joshua would be an invaluable resource for us and there were other resources mentioned. As a result, Julie accepted the responsibility of creating resource packets for us. A private social media account was established to host prayers concerns, praise, and items of interest. Robert and Bronson expressed ideas on how all could help as others offered suggestions. Others were mentioned as potential prayer partners and active participants. There's lots to do, but we're on the way. Several specific disciples were mentioned with their current situations and were lifted in fervent prayer. Robert also led one of the most intense, beautiful prayers I've ever heard, asking for God's blessing and direction. "Use us to reach souls for you, Lord. Give us the task and bless our actions that it glorify Your name."

GOD ANSWERS PRAYER

Saturday morning came and my phone rang. It was Robert. He was so excited. "Mama Kay, God took us seriously. He heard our prayers and answered. Within an hour of leaving your house my phone rang. It was Brandon Buddy reaching out. We went to get him from a hospital in Austin where he was released to the streets with nothing. Homeless, rejected, without anything! He's here! He's safe for now. Oh, God is good." But it wasn't time to celebrate yet.

Brandon is the wonderful young man and recent graduate whose story I shared with you. He was the object of our prayers the night before as the drama had already begun. How could this happen so quickly? I was so sure he was headed into a new life, but it didn't last long for one reason or another. I am again reminded of warnings offered at Oak Ridge graduations. "Be careful, be vigilant, the devil will be out to destroy you." How true!

Only the week before, someone had called Bronson saying that Brandon Buddy needed to be picked up at another hospital in Austin where he'd gone for help in detoxing. Bronson went, fed him, and took him home. All the while he tried to convince him to call the Ridge or Joshua, but shame had already taken hold of Brandon. The next day, Robert had gone to the house and called and called with no response. Others tried to contact Brandon, to no avail. But now, in answer to prayers, Brandon reached out to Robert. Thank you, Jesus.

The drama that began Friday night with Brandon continued. By noon, Robert called again saying they had Brandon at another hospital because of severe withdrawal and seizures. I went to relieve them that afternoon. We all prayed. As I sat by his bed and watched the now calm, sleeping man my mind wandered. I'd never seen severe withdrawal. Ironically, the closest I had come to seeing that was when Brandon himself had portrayed that role on a soap opera. I snickered, but truth was, it wasn't funny at all. I sat patiently, prayed, and exchanged conversation as he roused from sleep periodically. He was released later that day and I took him to my house. As we left the emergency room I asked, "Brandon, you're not going to run from me are you? I ask you because this old lady is in no shape to catch you." "No ma'am," he replied quietly, with downcast eyes. Later that evening Paul and I returned him to Robert's care. There were still lots of unknowns, but God would direct. Sunday went as Brandon slept and we wondered what was next. We even came up with tentative plans for the work week. Robert texted Coach—the nickname that the boys use for Joshua. At church on Sunday, Bronson talked to Joshua about Brandon. Joshua told him there was one bed open at the Ridge and ten men who wanted it. He said he'd give it to Brandon if he wanted to come. Still, we had questions, but God never missed a beat.

Now things began to unfold quickly. TJ called me on his way here from Dallas. He was coming for the Labor Day party for the disciples. He'd heard about Brandon and wanted to talk to him. Robert got Brandon up and ready to come to Sunday evening church service. Jordan, our young adult minister, was ready to encourage Brandon also. As we drove up we saw all the disciples piling out of the van and coming to the sanctuary. TJ arrived and greeted his brothers. Before long Joshua also entered the worship center. The stage was set and the Spirit of God was moving. It was a joy to watch it all happen. Brandon came in with Robert and Alicia and was greeted warmly by TJ. Very quickly, Joshua came back and sat down next to Brandon and TJ. Brandon wanted to be there but that first step to face others is ever so difficult. He sat calmly between the two spiritual leaders. Praise ensued and then the message. Alicia and Robert had joined Paul and me on the far side of the church. I have a feeling that my heart wasn't the only one thumping loudly as the Spirit of God moved. The service ended and we were quietly talking about what next when Joshua came rushing over. All I heard from Joshua were these words, "I'm going to scoop him up right now and take him to the Ridge. He's a dead man if I don't." I don't think I hollered "Hallelujah" but I don't know for sure. Tears began rolling down my face as I grabbed Joshua and hugged him, thanking him for his big Christian heart and willingness to help. That is the Joshua I know and love. That is the Joshua I have come to love and respect. Praise be to God! I am so blessed to have found that Bible and its owner. It's been an amazing journey thus far. The story continues. "Trust in the Lord with all your heart, and lean not on your own understanding; in all your ways acknowledge Him, and He will direct your paths" (Ps. 119: 10–11).

GREAT IS THY FAITHFULNESS

Great is Thy faithfulness, O God my Father;
There is no shadow of turning with Thee
Thou changest not, Thy compassions, they fail not
As Thou hast been, Thou forever wilt be
Pardon for sin and peace that endureth,
Thine own dear presence to cheer and to guide;
Strength for today, and bright hope for tomorrow,
Blessings all mine, with ten thousand beside.
Great is Thy faithfulness! Great is Thy faithfulness!
Morning by morning new mercies I see.
All I have needed Thy hand hath provided.
Great is Thy faithfulness, Lord unto me!

by Thomas Chisholm

FINAL THOUGHTS FROM THE AUTHOR

*T*his is God's story and I am blessed to share it. God is definitely in charge of events with His constant abiding love and direction. In sharp contrast to our God is our human nature, which often gets in the way of our relationship with our Savior. Above all, there is hope for all those who choose Him. My story encompasses events occurring over about eight years, starting with FINDING and KEEPING the Bible that was to lead me on a journey to discover LOSERS who became WINNERS in God's kingdom. It is a true recollection of events and people, though not necessarily sequential. Joshua and the ministry of Oak Ridge are indeed real.

My plea is that you become even more aware of God's presence and that you would follow His direction. Just pray and reach out. There is hope for every individual as God loves us all. Accept His gift of love as your Savior. May you always be led and blessed by our Heavenly Father.

"May the God of hope fill you with all joy and peace as you trust in Him, so that you may overflow with hope by the power of the Holy Spirit" (Rom. 15:13).

Special dedication to Tanner and others who have gone on to Heaven.

ACKNOWLEDGMENTS

I am filled with gratitude that my Heavenly Father would entrust me with this story to share. Special prayers of blessings to each reader accompany this book.

JOSHUA AND KAY

Joshua Harris and the Oak Ridge Disciple Ministry are central to the heart of this story; and, I am most grateful to God, who brought us together. Joshua will always hold a place of honor in my heart for his witness and his reliance on God. A special thanks to all of the many disciples, their families, and the supporters of Oak Ridge Disciple Ministry for so freely sharing your personal stories with me and allowing me to present them in print. I know your hearts and I know you yearn for others to find hope in Jesus.

OAK RIDGE FAMILY

Acknowledgments

DISCIPLE'S PRAYER CIRCLE

Sybille, loyal employee, without whom the Bible that led to this story would not have been found.

Paul, my best friend on earth, willingly became part of this journey. Your partnership has been unfailing.

JOSHUA, KAY, AND PAUL

May God continue to bless and extend the ministries of my church families at Crestview Baptist Church, First Baptist Church, Celebrate Recovery, and Oak Ridge Disciple Ministry, who played an integral part in this story.

I have been blessed by many prayer partners who took an active interest in sharing this message. Your support has been gratifying. Your encouragement has helped me tread this path of storytelling. Many of you took active roles of reading, editing, formatting, and everything else to develop this story of hope in God.

In this is my confidence, "God would have all men to be saved and come to the knowledge of the truth." (1 Timothy 2:4)

"Be strong and courageous! Do not be afraid or discouraged. For the Lord is with you wherever you go" (Josh. 19).

CONTACT INFORMATION

Kay Gray
lynkaygray@gmail.com
Facebook group: Finders Keepers Losers Winners
Kay is available for speaking engagements and often is accompanied by a disciple graduate.

Joshua Harris, Oak Ridge Ministry
PO Box 542 Florence, TX 76527
Phone: 512-905-2111
www.oakridgedisciplehouse.com
Oak Ridge Disciple House on YouTube

CPSIA information can be obtained
at www.ICGtesting.com
Printed in the USA
FSOW01n2037090516
20257FS